Howard Goldenberg is economist and anthropologist.

The World Now
The Spiral

Howard Goldenberg

Athamas
PRESS

Athens Auckland Bangkok Bogotá Buenos Aires Calcutta
Cape Town Chennal Dar es Salaam Delhi Florence Hong Kong Istanbul
Karachi Kuala Lumpur Madrid Melbourne Mexico City Mumbai
Nairobi Paris Shangai Singapore Taipei Tokyo Toronto Warsaw

and associated companies in
Valle Maggia Bar Uer I

First published by Athamas Press, 2014
298 Erhstest Ave, New York, NY 167822

ISBN-13:978-1500915506
ISBN-10:1500915505

Howard Goldenberg
The World Now - The Spiral
Includes text.

1. Economy. 2. Social Sciences. 3. Strategy.
II. Title.

Printed in the United States of America

This book is a collection of observations made in the year of 2013.

Howard Goldenberg

The World Now
The Spiral

Interconnection

Every day when we open the newspapers, we watch the news on TV, on the Internet, in any part of the the world, we are always surprised by a scenario of the most absolute contradictions. Old politicians, so often accused of corruption, placed in important public positions, in total impunity; young politicians criticizing the predecessors but tracing identical route, political lawmakers approving disastrous laws, and often in their favor; emerging opportunistic politicians, denouncing all that but willing to do the same; education getting worse; violence; new millionaires; bankruptcy of entire cities; higher taxes and more bureaucracy; new technologies of communication promising new standards of freedom; market manipulation and again general impunity; announcements of improvement of the economy; decrease of unemployment; but more and more miserable in the streets as well as in houses, and so on. But it does not happen only in the United States and yes all over the world. We have the historical habit of staying focused only on the United States without paying attention to other countries. But today, more than ever, everything is interconnected.

Focused on money

The problem of the manifest poor intellectual quality of governments, all over the world in general, is due to the fact that the political machine has developed a selection process favoring the worst, the less skilled, the unethical, but the most competent to defend their own interests, those for whom there are no limits to reach their objectives. Everything was transformed in the absolute goal of money, power, greed. But, a country, a society cannot be solely based on money. This may seem a contradiction, because we are used to associate business success to economic power, and consequently to the strengthening of a country. However, if we take the case of the United States as an example, we will see that its economic exuberance was not due to the groups that had on money their first and last goal. Instead, such groups that are intensely focused on money often meant barriers to development. John Nash mathematically proved it. What was decisive for the spectacular economic growth of the United States in the twentieth century - beyond the wars, turning possible an increasing Keynesian approach, and also generated by it - was the dream, the determination of people who had an objective and performed it. Such universe of invention and determination, freedom and courage, is blocked by the huge volume of laws and controls, by illiquidity, by high levels of taxes, and by the bureaucracy, which is arteriosclerotic par excellence. Such an atherosclerosis is generated by the ignorant, who believe to be able to control everything, to model the world, to regulate everything. The more ignorant a society is, the more it believes in bureaucracy as a civilizational value.

Preventive action

It is comprehensible that a society must have laws and regulations, but they must meet some essential principles: they must always be consistent with the Rule of Law; they should never block the flow of people's action; and they should always be set according to a posteriori criterium, never becoming an instrument of preventive action. All preventive action is economic noise.

Two

This story - which also involves the emergence of the imperialism of ignorance, nowadays present a little everywhere - is, in some sense, the history of the twentieth century. And, like in a play, it has its main characters. And it seems that they are two. Everything, even at the beginning of the twenty-first century, seems to have happened according to the conflict of two opposing and seemingly mutually exclusive trends: Hayek's monetarism and Keynes' paternalistic interventionism.

Good wave

Many people misunderstand this story - even politicians and journalists who advertise themselves as Keynesians believers. When they do that, they don't know Keynes - even considering that Keynes was brilliant. They are ignorant pretending and wishing be in the good wave.

Long term scenario

In 1923, Keynes said that when fixing the price of a currency taking gold as reference - which is the called "gold standard" - domestic prices will obligatorily fluctuate and could not be controlled. Thus, governments were forced to decide: either they would determine a currency with fixed value, a clear reference like the "gold standard", and had uncontrollable prices; or had a controlled currency and the domestic prices would not fluctuate so dramatically. Part of the present speculation on gold, performed by banks and financial institutions, adopted and approved by governments, is due to this desperate search of prices control. At that time, in the 1920s, the value of gold did not obey the principle of the market, but was determined by the bankers. Keynes was against the gold standard because it was controlled by the bankers and because he believed the State should control the value of the money. He believed that it would be possible in a long term scenario.

Prices control

Keynes established fundamental economic principles, in addition to having created what we call macro-economics. He established the principle according to which what determined the value of money was the speed of its use, not its quantity. Then, controlling the speed of capital circulation would be enough to obtain its control. And Keynes was in favor of prices control.

Market value

So, the Austrian economist Friedrich Hayek appears, who was totally against prices control. He said it was about a principle of freedom, a democratic principle. When a government ignores market prices and their fluctuations, when it controls them, it deprives individuals of their most important economic and democratic contribution to society: to express through their buying decision, their opinion about the true value of a product or service. This would determine the so-called "market value".

Strong opposition

Thus, for Hayek, governments should correct their public accounts, have small debt, low taxes, and let civil society be free to create wealth. However, the so-called "economic cycles" seem always exist in such a scenario of economic freedom. And here, especially, a strong opposition between Keynes and Hayek emerges.

Cycles

For Hayek, "economic cycles" are inevitable, and governments should let societies pass by them naturally, even if that would imply periods of great impoverishment. Keynes, on the other hand, considered unacceptable that phases of impoverishment could dramatically affect the poorest and argued that governments should borrow in periods of adverse economic cycles in order to protect the poorest and even the economy itself at a later stage of recovery. Thus, Keynes was considered a leftist politician - because he was reportedly worried about the poor; and Hayek, someone from the right wing, because he advocated a free economy, even if at certain times the poor would suffer.

Deeper disaster

There was another important factor. Some economists believed that depending on the frequency of the economic cycles, everything could enter into a downward spiral, without a State intervention, leading to total destruction. On the other hand, Hayek argued that everything naturally tended to equilibrium; and said that when the State intervenes, it eliminates the natural factor of strengthening of the economy, leading to an even deeper disaster after some time.

Pushed into war

Keynes argued that the State should intervene, borrowing up as it could, but that the product of the loans should be applied especially in roads, public works and social housing. According to his reasoning, taxes on consumption of people in those same works, associated with the elimination of quotas of population receiving unemployment benefits, would pay the loans and would even generate surplus results for the State, which could be reapplied in other public works. Hayek did not believe in this possibility. He thought that the debt would only increase, leading the country to bankruptcy and hence its loss of sovereignty. In such a process, facing to bankruptcy and loss of sovereignty, surely the country would be pushed into war.

Collective intelligence

Keynes believed that State intervention was essential precisely to preserve the freedom of individuals, who should seek profit. He did not believe in individual freedom in economic terms. As everything was connected, it would be impossible to think of freedom and independence. Everything was interdependent. He considered that many individuals were naturally ignorant or too weak, without power of decision, without even a social awareness. Thus, the State should intervene. On the other hand, Hayek believed that the sum of individual decisions would design a kind of collective intelligence.

1714

Keynes went further defending the Paradox of Saving, also known as Paradox of Thrift. Keynes would even argue that those who saved was working against nation, arguing that savings should be eliminated even if this required the use of force. The Paradox of Saving is based on old medieval tales and even from classical antiquity, and was popularized in the early eighteenth century by Bernard de Mandeville, poet, philosopher and politician born in the Netherlands but who lived much of his life in England. Bernard Mandeville became famous - and hated by many - thanks to his literary work "The Fable of the Bees: or, Private Vices, Publick Benefits", published in 1714.

Lives

Mandeville believed that human goodness and what we call ethical behavior were mere inventions and pure fantasies of politicians, with the aim of controlling social relations. Thus, according to him, everyone should work for his own interest, even if that would harm others. Only a society where some devoured others is that its economic relations would be stimulated. While for Adam Smith self-interest is always inevitably associated, in one way or another, to the common good; to Mandeville, it is through destruction and vice and that collective benefit emerges. A spendthrift psychopath, for example, spending lots of money on silly things, but such nonsense would result in spending that would move the society, even if lives, representing lower consumption, could be destroyed in such process.

Paradox of Saving

The Paradox of Saving argues that if people spare during times of crisis, this will cause to be less money in circulation, and therefore the value of money will decrease, reducing the amount of savings. That is, the person saves, removing the value from circulation, and so he will have less money because his savings will be worth less.

Inevitable

Keynes argued that the total incomes, of demand, should be equal to the total output; and the total investment should be equal to the total savings. In the moment the savings surpass the investment, the balance would be broken and the disaster would be inevitable: a new negative phase of the economic cycle would being generated.

Zero

Paul Krugman amplified that concept in The Paradox of Debt, because if the debt cannot be lower than the savings, and the savings increase, then the government will be forced to increase debt, thereby increasing taxes. Again here, the scale is forgotten. Of course, if all citizens hide all money, the debt will increase in an asymptotic curve. But, following the same reasoning, if people spend everything turning savings to zero, the debt should also be equal to zero, and it doesn't work like that. What shows the fallacy of his argumentation.

Recession

Hayek and others criticized the Paradox of Saving following some interesting reasonings. Firstly, if there is a crisis and people are saving more, there will exist less money in the market, and prices will fall due to decreased demand. When it happens, the lower prices will boost the economy, heating it again - this is the called Say's Law. On the other hand, Keynesians deny Say's Law, saying that prices do not necessarily fall during periods of recession.

Reserves

Not only, savings would not cause illiquidity, because that money would be in the banks, and the role of banks is to reinvest in society. So, the more people would save their economies, more money for loans would be injected into society. That would not happen only if, for some reason, the money was spared in cash by individuals or banks would not reinvest it, generating a growth of excess reserves.

Gold

In a certain sense, it is also what is happening now with gold. Because of the elimination of all forms of saving, many people around the world - and many States like China for example - is buying physical gold. Then, banks and financial institutions - covered by governments - started issuing a huge quantity of gold certificates without financial backing. But, both types of gold - physical and certificates are quoted as part of the same thing. But they are not! So, gold is openly manipulated - with the approval of authorities of all kinds.

Banks

Anyway, the Paradox of Saving can only happen in closed economies. In open economies, the exports may counteract the paradox because if in an economy between two countries, for example, the trade balance is unbalanced, the part that buys more than sells eliminates savings and decreases its domestic liquidity; while the part that sells more than buys rises savings and increases domestic liquidity - considering that saving money is reinvested by banks.

Freedom

Moreover, the elimination of savings destroys a fundamental social element: the inter-generational solidarity. The elimination of savings creates a population of dependents, a population without power of reaction against unjust and tyrannical governments, and a population of oppressed and kidnapped. The elimination of savings is a terrible threat to individual freedom.

Confiscation

The same governments that persecute citizens with an overwhelming bureaucracy, unprecedented fiscal terrorism, and establish all mechanisms of confiscation and elimination of savings are largely composed - according to articles published in newspapers around the world - by politicians who became millionaires thanks to the public money, and that are always unpunished.

Asymmetry

In several countries, such as Brazil or the United States, for example, a person who has any inconsistency in their tax data - even without any debt to the State - automatically loses his civil rights. And this is a scandalous asymmetry between State and Nation.

Utility

Hayek, and the entire Austrian School, believed that productivity was not determined by the amount of money, or even by its velocity of circulation, but yes by the balance between consumption and investment. When people lack confidence in the economy, buy more money. That is, they prefer the utility of money, as a safeguard for survival, that the utility of goods and services.

Spiral

Then, the equation is set up on both sides. For Austrians, if demand and prices fall at equal levels, productivity will be maintained, because the relation between price and consumption will remain equivalent. In some critical moments, Hayek came to agree with the usefulness of Keynes position, but not in a generalized way. On the other hand, Keynesians argue that if prices fall and productivity remain the same, also with lower demand, as Austrian economists claim, then incomes will also decrease. This change will inevitably lead, according to them, to the expectation of deflation, making people stop buying today hoping for better prices tomorrow, and leading to a downward spiral and the resulting catastrophe.

Crisis

The essential question in this entire discussion is to know whether or not the government should invest contracting debt in times of crisis. There are certain factors that were apparently left behind by Keynes. Public investment in order to avoid crises by eliminating - even partially - the negative phases of the economic cycles will only work if meet certain assumptions. Firstly, there can be no corruption. If governments inflate the values of projects in order to benefit - as newspapers have generously denounced around the world over the past several decades and in many different countries - nothing will be possible, and the debt will naturally be suicidal and odious.

Average

Still, as Keynes argued, these investments should not compete with private enterprise. If generalized, they tend to eliminate productive sectors. Thus, they should be focused especially in the sectors whose internal logic does not obey to the Principle of Average - as it happens in much of the productive fabric in capitalist societies. Health and education, for example, operate internally logical systems of different natures.

Making no sense

Regarding the money taken by the government, the

interest rate should be relatively low, at least below the growth of the economy. If the interest rate is above the level of economic growth, the loans will never be paid - unless the country dispose its assets, but then it would be making equity transfer and the loans would make no sense.

Inflation

In relation to the money invested in segments whose internal logic does not obey the Principle of Average - the interest rate should be slightly above inflation and below an index generated by a combination of inflation and economic growth.

Interest rates

On the other hand, interest rates cannot be floating - because floating rates prevent any planning. Still, widespread lending to the private sector must comply with stable criteria. A system of suicide-loans would be of no use to the country, because they are a priori impossible to get paid! The interest rates on such loans should be neither too high nor too low - depending on the country. The calculation shall include the estimated industry growth. The government, in any case, should not forget that it is a public service and not an organ of fiscal terrorism.

GDP

None of this will make sense if the GDP calculation is flawed and corrupt with the inclusion of data contrary to their functions - such as the widespread inclusion of public expenditure as income! Moreover, no State investment could also reverse the economic crisis under an intense bureaucracy.

Bureaucracy

Bureaucracy can be useful in small doses. Larger doses asphyxiate any economy, representing a huge cost not only in terms of taxes, but also in fixed costs of the companies. All this means less tax revenues and catastrophe.

Citizens

More than that, bureaucracy generates a growing social asymmetry, benefiting large groups and harming citizens.

Crisis

Another problem that undermines the Keynesian thesis is the degree of openness of the country. If the country is part of a open international trade network, as it is established by the WTO, then investments in one country can be transferred to another. That is, the taxes of a country will pay benefits to another country. It is the case of companies that received investment and were sold below their market value, to another country in a time of crisis.

War

And what is even more terrible: the increasing process established by the Keynesian model leads to a increasing need of money and, consequently, to war.

Very well

What we witness, informed by the newspapers every day, in different countries, are scandals involving governors who get rich or that make richer third parties - of course, with public money, and that apparently are untouchable and unpunished; the manipulation of GDP values; open economies applying Keynesian principles; investments in economic areas that cannibalize other ones; floating interest rates; odious contracts. Anyway, in such a scenario, nothing can work very well.

Totalitarian regimes

Recent history tells us how, under the pressure of the United States, China joined the WTO in 2001 in a condition that is not consistent with its internal reality. Large groups of interests sought to relocate their production to China, which is a country of slavery nature, a dictatorial and totalitarian regime, with no courts, almost without lawyers, where Law is improvised by the political party, which is only one.

Inflation

The relocation of production also relocated liquidity deeply affecting Western countries. On the other hand, the dramatic expansion of the monetary basis do not put all money in the market, but remained a process controlled by the banks and governments. In this way, even if it there is a tremendous expansion, it doesn't entirely affect inflation, at least until now.

Mao

The argumentation in favor of the integration of China, as it was done, was that it would lead to an inevitable opening of the country and to a strong improvement of the conditions of the population and to democratization. However, what we saw in the last almost fifteen years has been the explosion of a terrible social asymmetry, of censorship - which controls even the speeches of the President of the United States - and a picture of devastating corruption that reminds the times before Mao Zedong - and more importantly, the continuity of a scenario where the slavery regime, with symbolic if not miserable wages, no employment rights, no rights to health and education, with a generalization of mafia structures, did not finish, by contrary.

Liquidity

This complex scenario provoked two pernicious things: produced a dramatic reduction in liquidity; and invaded the Western capitalist markets with radically cheap products - because they are the result of slave labor. It was believed that the dramatic reduction in liquidity resulting from the relocation of production would be balanced with an intense expansion of the monetary basis and its consequent inflationary pressure. By its turn, in a complex equation, the inflationary trend would be compensated by the invasion of very cheap goods, whose pressure is deflationary. But the scale of China is so overwhelming and its regime is so determinedly despotic and tyrannic, that the deflationary pressure far exceeded that expansion of the monetary basis.

Sky

So, there is a dilemma: if governments and banks inject great quantities of money in the market, it can generate an inflationary spiral, and the debits will go to the sky. If they continue concentrating the expansion of the monetary basis in internal fluxes, the depression will go deeper and a destruction of the production system will happen. And the latter is the scenario created in the Western countries.

Stagdeflation

Thus, the West entered into a crisis of stagnation associated with a deflationary trend, what we could call stagdeflation - no longer the famous picture of stagflation of the 1970s. To offset this black board, economists from around the world, especially from the largest universities, integrated in governments, often corrupt, began to defend a Keynesian framework to save the world economy.

Invasion

Thus, to balance the deflationary pressure, monetary base was increased - but inflation levels have remained relatively stable, with a tendency to deflation. To compensate the economic paralysis, especially around 2008, massive public investments were made. In 2003 the Iraq war happened. France has heavily invested in its auto industry and private companies - against the law. The United States too. Other disguised war was the called Arab Spring. But with the continuous and rapid increase of the monetary base, combined with public investment, the public debt exploded - leading to a general increase in taxes, sometimes disguised here and there. This caused a further decrease liquidity, but the deflationary pressure continued augmenting thanks to the invasion of goods produced with slaves.

Banks

Since then, governments passed to eliminate all forms savings. But that too was not enough. So, now they passed to eliminate existing savings through the open manipulation of gold, the imposition of negative interests, manipulation of stock markets and so on - resulting in a clear strategy of confiscation. Today, like in 1920, in fact, the banks are determining again the value of gold, through the immense issue of certificates, with suspicious lack of concrete reference.

Freedom

Negative interests, increase of taxes, elimination all forms of savings, all kinds of manipulation - including of information - and increase of bureaucracy represent tools of confiscation. We should never forget that the United States was born because of the firmly determination in the defense of freedom, against high taxes, in favor of democratic representation, and in favor of savings. Now, the planet is entirely covered by human beings. Would we be witnessing the end of the last place of freedom on Earth?

Common market

The United States plans to build a large common market together with Europe, but imposing its model of development. An European standardization following the American model would imply the end of the European social model - whose aims were similar to the American ones when of the foundation of the United States.

Impossible to be paid

In the last years, and tremendously quickly, specially after 2001 and the Iraq war in 2003, the position of the United States became fragile. Its industry was in great part substituted by the Chinese. Many consider the US debt simply impossible to be paid. Its expansion of the monetary basis is tremendous, but not only it has been concentrated in banks, as its inflationary pressure has been, at least since 1947, absorbed by the fact that dollar was transformed into an international currency for business after Bretton Woods. However, there are strong rumors that China, India and Brazil are organizing a new central bank, to create a new currency, in substitution of the dollar.

Pressure

China continues its exploitation of slave labor and environmental destruction. If there is a social crisis in China, the inflationary pressure in the West will be explosive and devastating.

Who will break first

All this scenario of pressures, plunged into conditions that annul the benefits of Keynesian interventions, also responds to a geostrategic principle: the dramatic reduction of liquidity in the West would lead to a crisis without inflation, but with great reduction in consumption, leading China to an inevitable democratization. But China's resilience has proved worthy of the ferocious regime that imposes violent censorship, control of the citizens, and summary condemnations - including death penalty - without trials. The question that sometimes arises is to know who will break first.

Slave labor

The West has not broke yet because is surviving thanks to the slave labor of millions of Chinese.

Surveillance

This situation hides another danger. With the elimination of savings, any potential of popular resistance against a dictatorial regime is greatly weakened and, in many cases, simply eliminated. Especially if you have in mind the surveillance systems at all levels, and the growing bureaucracy, which is also an important factor of control and surveillance.

Lawyers

The elimination of the savings are another phenomenon - people are driven, often without realizing it,
to desperately seek the largest profit in everything
they do. Everything passes to be a hunting for money, as a sovereign value of the society. Research or
culture pass to be much less important. Before, a
teacher or a director os a school, for example, were
deeply respected people. Students and parents had
a manifested respect for their works. Now, they are
treated as obsolete elements in society. In the same
way, medicine, which was once a public service, has
become a nightmare for many, causing generalized
fear because of the astronomical prices, many times
unjustifiable; the schools, which were also a place
of public service, became a place for production of
criminals, specially when dealing with many schools
for the poorest, or in an unjustifiable commerce with
astronomical prices. In general, one could say the
same about architects, dentists or even of great part
of lawyers.

Service

Such mentality, to which the elimination of savings
contributes decisively, also seems to be that of the
rulers, in their most varied functions - and they too
once belonged to the category of public service.

Fiscal terrorism

Of course, with an intense bureaucracy, with a fiscal terrorism of State, consequent low metabolism, of course high debts, the demagogic always arrive with the pretense and false solution of more taxes. It is preferable more taxes than austerity, they say - but no one says that killing the economy, more taxes will represent nothing; and no one says about corruption and the new aristocracy that invaded and conquered the planet.

Fiction

Apparently, we all became dominated by all-powerful, ignorant and incompetent bureaucrats - when they are not thieves. They often seem to be completely lost, but convinced to be omniscient beings, true geniuses, forged in halls of social gatherings and in the theories pertaining to the realm of fiction, seeming to believe to be the saviors of the world. Exactly as it had happened with Hitler, Mussolini, Stalin or Mao Zedong.

Consumption and fun

Such world of apparent widespread incompetence, of immense social inequalities, of unexplained and unacceptable thefts against large population contingents, of manifested impunity, where the Rule of Law seems to be rapidly disintegrating, reminds us of Aldous Huxley when he said that "the perfect dictatorship have the appearances of democracy, a prison without walls in which prisoners do not even will dream with the escape. A system of slavery where, thanks to consumption and fun, the slaves will love their servitude".

Articulation

When we look at the world map, or at one of those wonderful nocturnal planetary images by NASA, we often think about how places on Earth, peoples, societies and institutions articulate themselves. To this, to such "articulation" of societies, we call "strategy": the approach of action to achieve an end, a goal. We often attribute strategy as role of governments, and we forget that the world is dynamic. All strategy is, by its very nature, teleological - something that seeks something else. We find in Machiavelli's Prince a powerful representation of this process. When there is not military, all strategy essentially is economic.

Future

From the smallest to the most powerful countries, strategy is almost always present. But it is also permeated by strategies established by interest groups and powerful institutions such as the Pentagon, the

IMF or the World Bank for example. The diversity of strategic principles in planetary terms is not only fascinating but also establishes an intriguing scenario that unveils a hidden present and leads to a probable future... only probable.

Scandal

The United States, through intelligence centers such as the Pentagon, seem to establish clear and identifiable strategic principles. They seem to be based on the control of all flows in the world - what basically is control on information and transportation. Thus, all seas and oceans of the planet are currently controlled by the United States, like what happens with virtually all air space. On communication, much before the appearance of the scandal regarding the controversial role of the NSA, everyone already knew the Echelom Project. The fact that this scandal appeared only in 2013 seems, in fact, to be a strategic event.

Wars

Other side of the American strategic reality is present in the fact that the country no longer need to make wars to control regions. The difference in military power is so huge that just throwing bombs breaking the delicate balance of the concerned region is enough. This does not mean that the United States does not need wars, but at the beginning of the 21st century such need became exclusively economic:

how to feed the country's economic system. This is another information about its strategic design.

Participation

Participation in the economies of other countries, especially in Europe, is another data about the American strategic structure. On the other hand, after the Second World War, the United States appear to also dominate, ever more intensely, the European political scene. Europe represents a geo-strategic importance to the United States, since it works as a sort of base of operations for Asia and the Middle East.

Corridors

There are certain special "corridors", like the "energy corridors" and the "flow corridors", in the planet. The region linking China to the Central Asia, more specifically to the Caspian Sea, is an "energy corridor" - because the huge production of oil and gas - as well as the Mediterranean coast of Turkey to Israel - because of the strategic transportation and production of oil. The Gulf of Hormuz and the China Seas are two important "flow corridors". Sometimes, flow and energy are mixed in the corridors. And , the most important "flow corridor" is the orbital space, currently almost entirely dominated by the United States. These "corridors" are important because they can choke streams if disrupted. In the case of orbital space, it gives whoever dominates the power to control all regions of Earth.

Himalayas

There are also strategic points like the Himalayas, the Alps, or the Amazon Basin, because the water production. This is the reason Tibet was invaded by China, because it depends on water from the Himalayas.

Points and Corridors

These "points" and "corridors" that are physical elements, started being articulated in the new reality of cyberspace. In the virtual space-time, everything becomes more unstable and volatile. But the United States is not the only country to have a strategic vision on a global level. There are also China and Russia.

Three strategic areas

China clearly has some strategic purposes: to develop a very efficient and aggressive army; to develop a powerful navy especially to control the seas of China; and dominate the orbital space. In these three strategic areas, their ambitions are directly conflicting with American interests.

Three strategic elements

On the other hand, China seems to have another level of strategic performance. In virtually all countries with which it has established business relations, Chinese seek to purchase sources of water and electricity (and its distribution) and telecommunications systems. In Africa and Brazil, in addition to these three elements, they are also focused on commodities. In the United States, the Chinese made the relocation of industrial production a trap - in exchange for exorbitant profits, thanks to the Chinese slave labor, the importation of products made in slavery-oriented countries is annihilating the U.S. real economy. A country threatened by its own greed! This happens not only with the United States - is exactly the same in Europe, Africa or Brazil. It is not enough to be a very rich country if its wealth does not circulate in the economy.

Paradox

In seeking to control the Maghreb, North Africa, China seems to have funded terrorist groups - also in the "energy corridor" of the Pakistan and Afghanistan which leads to Iran and therefore to the Caspian Sea. It is an apparent paradox, because for decades China has fought against Islamic radicals in its western regions. The American response, sometimes badly "disguised" by apparent European initiatives, sparked attacks on Libya and unchained the Arab Spring - apparently orchestrated through electronic systems and with a strange logic to that region (but absolutely typical in a literate culture), and also attempted attack on Syria.

Depletion

On the other hand, apparently the policy of forced illiquidity - ie depletion - both in Europe and in the United States would have been a strategic resource in order to crush the Chinese economy, leading to social unrest and to a democratization of the country. Thus, while China would be acting outside of its country, the United States would be acting within China.

Russia

There is also Russia - small with immense territory, aged population - establishing subtle strategic ties with China, quiet negotiations again around the Caspian Sea, a few words about Afghanistan, and the defense of its largest military port abroad: Syria.

Dynamics

But strategic issues are dynamic in nature. A dictatorial regime - and especially in China dimensions - has a high level of resistance. In a place where the killings perpetrated by the State, summary killings even without the right to trial, are considered normal, the energy needed for social change is much greater. But in both the United States and in Europe, open systems, this energy is much smaller.

Chinese army

Strategic issues are extremely dynamic. According to Anthony Harrington, an award-winning business and energy journalist, the very expansion of the Chinese military, as it has been made, may have been product of the United States itself, through its armaments industry. Thus, China would have invested in expanding its army to control their own populations and boundaries, giving the control of the legitimacy of the waters to the United States. But, as Harrington says, China is tightly controlled by the military and radical speeches are not rare. In any case, while the Chinese strategic approach seems to produce a stable pattern; Western strategic vision is subject to the fluctuations of individual interests. For example: the United States and Europe establish a strategy of crushing its own economy as a way to strangle the Chinese economy, dependent on the consumption of manufactured goods. But on the other hand, China - or countries that formerly was called "fourth-world" - provides even cheaper conditions for the sale of its manufactured products to American and European populations, and suddenly, everything changes.

Redcaps

And the Western pressures start - in northern France, the redcaps go down streets and roads claiming their former purchasing power, devastated by the disastrous performance of the European Union. In the United States, entire towns no longer have street lighting, libraries or museums, for lack of money. In New York City, De Blasio, who self-proclaims the avenger of the poor and righteous, won the elections for mayor with an overwhelming majority, promising to pursue the rich on behalf of the poor. Who could imagine such a thing in a city like Manhattan? Sometimes I'm amazed at how it is common to see demagogic proposals such as "Robin Wood" actions that are never realized (and when they are, they produce fabulous disasters), but its is almost never proposed to improve the condition of the poor, through more education and development opportunities. It seems to always be "the grass is always greener on the other side of the fence" syndrome.

Regulations and corruption

In Europe, the EU administration - apparently totally controlled by the U.S. administration - constituted a bastion of bureaucratic aristocrats, spreading all sorts of regulations and rules, aiming to control everything, even the privacy of individuals and thus blocking even more the already poor European economy. Worse, it has also happened in the United States. This is a true economic arteriosclerosis in its beginning.

Frauds and aristocracy

Moreover, another phenomenon has emerged: all types of institutional frauds started - like the GDP, the inflation and so on. Numbers, even defended by leading experts of the most renowned universities in the world... which are but lies. Because of ignorance or interests most of the media is silent on this scenario. The index of corruption seems to have fired - although many statistics show otherwise. EU officials receive high salaries, are always covered with unexplained benefits, even VAT they do not pay. An aristocracy that revolt good people. And the populations of free societies manifest accordingly to what they live. France passed to be described as the stage of a hidden civil war, which is denied, disguised. The same happens in other countries, but not in totalitarian regimes.

Two natures

Thus, the United States and Europe are obliged to change and redesign their strategy almost continuously. Then strategy seems to give place to tactic. After the 1980s, American and European real economies were transformed into economies of debt, disintegrating the purchasing power and savings. The gulf between State and Nation became even more evident. Especially European people, that do not belong to the despotic Chinese tradition, have in their imaginary work and savings as the core social elements - and are alarmed because they disappeared. Another element of this imaginary are the banks, with their ancient social function, which was born, in fact, in medieval Europe - it was also annihilated. In the United States, the social composition is rapidly changing with the integration of millions of Latin Americans, Africans, Arabs and from other countries without a strong literary and therefore democratic tradition. The same also happens in Europe but, excepting France, there the scale of this phenomenon is smaller and the literary sedimentation in European countries is still high. The U.S. made a huge historical mistake to surreptitiously prolong the African slavery through a quasi-apartheid that lasted until the early 1970s. A mistake that could cost the country's future. Even today, the American cinema is strongly racist - very rarely, almost never, we see couples and families formed by different races in American movies. In them, blacks marry blacks, whites marry whites and Asians marry Asians.

Manipulation

Today, the level of final taxation reaches more than 70% of the people resources, eliminating the purchasing power. Interest rates are negative, not only eliminating savings but also promoting a true confiscation. Politicians formed a caste of untouchables - for many in both senses of the term. The pressure of public opinion is a vital element in strategic decision-making in Western countries - therefore the manipulation of information has become increasingly intense.

Ad Absurdum

But strategic ways happen at different scales - including mentalities. Many Chinese, for example, are buying land well located in touristic European cities, and they are building hotels just for Chinese, with restaurants and shops also for Chinese. So, Chinese tourists are greeted at airports by Chinese, transferred to the Chinese hotels by other Chinese, eat and consume only in Chinese shops and restaurants, practically consuming nothing from the place and not participating in life of the city - working in a closed circuit. Chinese already made at least two of such big hotels in Venice, Italy, and the population - than before considered them a bit closed - deeply miss of the American tourists. Doing that, Chinese disrespect the local population, use the city for their business, excluding other people - what is not a democratic tradition. In an ad absurdum exercise, if such continues and spread out, local populations will be transformed in slaves for Chinese tourists.

Strange reason

In Portugal, millionaires linked to the Angolan dictator Jose Eduardo Dos Santos, are literally buying the country. Incidentally, Angolan millionaires bought even Ferrari! - a country where dictatorship is as violent as their already famous level of corruption. I remember when, years ago, President George W. Bush accused the Angolan dictator to be corrupt. The answer came quickly: Dos Santos replied that it was Bush who was corrupt. For some strange reason, nothing happened.

Demography

If anyone says that the world is experiencing a demographic implosion among the most cultivated and educated populations; and a demographic explosion among the ignorant and miserable - he may be correct, but is politically incorrect and will surely be accused of being a fascist.

Corruption

If you say that great part of today's politicians - and their accomplices such as many businessmen, union leaders, journalists and teachers - especially from important universities - are true bandits, you will surely be accused of being antidemocratic and, again, even fascist. But the truth is that in virtually all countries of the world the political universe is rotten and representative democracy has become a very effective weapon to steal millions of people with the most peaceful and absolute impunity. It is organized crime. But when that accusation is made evident every day, through news in newspapers, sometimes outrageously flattering, there is no reaction from the population. Some believe that people is in fear. Others believe that everyone is paralyzed. Those who denounce such things are called "incendiary." However, if we will not be able to renew the democratic process, liberating it from criminals, it will die and will be substituted by tyranny.

Crime

The same politicians who took the devastating debts, often in association with criminal banks and companies, condemning generations of citizens who did not give them power to do so, are the same who are now in power in institutions that crush these same populations! They transformed collective institutions into criminal syndicates. No one manifests against it. To manifest in such sense is politically incorrect, because it would indicate that the person doesn't believe in democracy.

IMF

In an International Monetary Fund report of October 2013 it is written that "the sharp deterioration of the public finances in many countries has revived interest in a 'capital levy' — a one-off tax on private wealth — as an exceptional measure to restore debt sustainability. The appeal is that such a tax, if it is implemented before avoidance

is possible and there is a belief that it will never be repeated, does not distort behavior (and may be seen by some as fair). There have been illustrious supporters, including Pigou, Ricardo, Schumpeter, and — until he changed his mind — Keynes. The conditions for success are strong, but also need to be weighed against the risks of the alternatives, which include repudiating public debt or inflating it away (these, in turn, are a particular form of wealth tax — on bondholders — that also falls on nonresidents).

As for instance in Bach (There is a surprisingly large amount of experience to draw on, as such levies were widely adopted in Europe after World War I and in Germany and Japan after World War II. Reviewed in Eichengreen (1990), this experience suggests that more notable than any loss of credibility was a simple failure to achieve debt reduction, largely because the delay in introduction gave space for extensive avoidance and capital flight — in turn spurring inflation.

The tax rates needed to bring down public debt to precrisis levels, moreover, are sizable: reducing debt ratios to end-2007 levels would require (for a sample of 15 euro area countries) a tax rate of about 10 percent on households with positive net wealth." It is deeply impressive how someone can write a thing like that! The text assumes that to compensate the sharp deterioration of the public finances the State should confiscate savings! But such a tool never ever solved any problem of public finances. By contrary, when applied it always affected negatively the situation of the country, eliminating credibility and destroying economy. The author of the IMF text even underlines that the appeal is that such a tax, if it is implemented before avoidance

is possible and there is a belief that it will never be repeated, does not distort behavior (and may be seen by some as fair)! Apparently suggesting that it is an efficient way to cheat the citizens... there is a belief that it will never be repeated... and may be seen by some as fair. Unbelievable how such an institution still exists! But if someone manifests himself against it, will be accused to be against progress and help to poor countries - even if, apparently, in its entire history the IMF have never saved any country from misery.

Communication

Several books and articles have been constantly published denouncing the IMF, the World Bank and other entities as extensions of the military world industry. There are also accusations that the political world in various nations is directly involved in global drug trafficking - which is an extremely lucrative business. Accusations are made, evidences arise, but everything seems to be constantly blocked by groups of interest that, in one way or other, dominate journalism in general. Who says that will automatically be classified as conspiratorial, negative spirit and anti-capitalist.

Bureaucracy

The world is becoming more and more bureaucratic. Bureaucracy is not only a mechanism of distribution of capital to unskilled people but also an efficient system of transference of large amounts of capital to big corporations, and also a process of market reserve for those same corporations. The cost of bureaucracy for a single person is the same for a company with fifteen thousand people; so, it is absolutely unequal in proportions. In this way, because of bureaucracy costs, it is not permitted to a single person or to a group of few people to enter in the market, intensifying social asymmetry; whereas bureaucracy represents virtually no cost to large corporations. But if someone says that, will be accused to be anti-democratic because bureaucracy is, as fraudulent artifice, commonly described as an instrument for the safeguard of the conditions of social equity in individual rights.

Education

The level of education is getting worse in the world. In several countries, such as Brazil for instance, school failure became in many cases prohibited by law. Studying or not, having or not knowledge, all students are obliged to automatically pass to the next academic year. This produces an immense mass of ignorant people who will be unable to manage their own destiny in the future. However a true crime against the future of a nation, such law is great to create and freeze a permanent army of slave labor; and it is also a great way to fill official statistics with beautiful numbers. Who is contrary to that will be accused of being elitist, of being someone against the people, against the poorest... when what happens is exactly the opposite.

Yuppies

In the early 2010s, there is a sensation of resurgence of a new wave of yuppies - the same kind of people that devastated the planet in the 1980s and 1990s. They are ignorant youth with no connection to society, selfish greedy competitors working exclusively to themselves, well behaved in appearance, arrogant growers of their own egos, manipulators and speculators who are there to destroy who will be in their way. Of course, under the guise of successful entrepreneurs, leaving a trail of destruction and poverty behind, they are not intelligent - as so brilliantly it was mathematically demonstrated by John Nash. But no one complains, as well as no one denounces the increasing amount of financial groups whose sole purpose is theft. Talking about it is taboo even if, in fact, they are all criminals, gangsters.

Pharmaceutical industry

Everyday global pharmaceutical industry is accused of all kinds of fraud and cartels among many other types of serious crimes. Journalistic works show that drugs we often use as medicine contain substances other than those indicated in their compositions. But it is also true that pharmaceutical industry is extremely powerful and, so, there is hardly any reaction against it. When a reaction happens, in general it is about a scandal due to conflict between interest groups, but almost never something for the protection of the consumer. Whoever will denounce it will be accused exactly of the opposite: to be defending some obscure interest and may be, also here, politically incorrect.

Kyoto Treaty

The world economy is destroying the planet - especially after both George W. Bush and Barack Obama administrations have virtually condemned the Kyoto Treaty to disappearance. That's what many scientific studies show every week. Almost extinct species of fish and animals, an unprecedented rise in global temperature, heavy metals deposited on the seabed, part of Asia already permanently covered by toxic clouds... unfortunately, the examples are many and diversified. This reality represents a monstrous economic cost - not to say other ones - for future generations. But if someone denounces it, will immediately be labeled as reactionary and against development.

Environmentalists

On the other hand, many environmentalists argue that we all should immediately abandon everything and start living as it was customary in the Middle Ages, in name of planetary sustainability - what is a tremendous absurd. If it should be like that we should also abandon penicillin, antibiotics, scientific discoveries that made possible a fabulous increase in life expectancy and a dramatic decrease in infant mortality. Here too, if someone denounces such absurd, will be immediately classified as a reactionary unethical capitalist and therefore will be deeply politically incorrect.

Cities

Cities are becoming true monstrosities, losing their former "urban" condition. Today, great part of the people living in large megacities are not "urban," they have no "civility", they are worse than animals, without culture, with very low standards of hygiene, ignorant, true semi-animal slaves kept in open captivity in the form of outdoors sewage. Although they are victims, immersed in a world of horror, misery, disease and violence, those who denounce such hateful situation will immediately be accused of prejudice against that same people, because political correctness is the aesthetics of poverty. "Urban" became classified as backward and "bourgeois."

Cities 2

Still in relation to the cities, many of them have being systematically destroyed by their own governors. Madrid and New York City are two quite illustrative examples of this phenomenon. In New York City taxes and duties have been established by the administration in such magnitude in the last several years that much of the traditional population was replaced by young ignorant speculators, eliminating the ancient culture of the city. Not only, the blind imposition of intense and voracious taxation virtually eliminated the diversity of the commercial fabric of the city - forcing the closure of bookstores, music stores, art galleries or small business specialized in niche markets. So, walking today in the famous Fifth Avenue in New York City is practically the same as being at any avenue on the periphery of Caracas, Venezuela. But no one says that. Everything is covered by the politically correct and in this case the rule is to say, irresponsibly and demagogically, that everyone must be subjected to a same huge tax burden because it is on behalf of the entire community. This is false, because such actions seriously undermines the collectivity.

Gold

2013 indicators seem to show that there is a huge speculation regarding the commercialization of gold - focused on manipulation of certificates. This causes a terrible imbalance in the market and a formidable concentration of resources by large corporations and States, eliminating one of the last features for savings - all others have already been eliminated. The manipulation of certificates has been constantly denounced as a work of criminal corporations and venal States. Curiously, who denounces it will be accused to be a speculator!

Health

Do you live in a building? Try to administrate it yourself: you will be very impressed with a successful, sudden and dramatic fall of all charges and costs. Why? Because everyone involved in the professional administration of buildings - and it seems be true also about everything - often is oriented to make money for themselves, as fast as possible. And you pay for it. The same happens with good part of doctors, in several countries. I've many friends, rich people in rich cities that avoid as much as possible to visit a doctor. They say that visiting a doctor, even in a routine check-up, would represent to be faced to a very expensive bill, to non-necessary exams, to lack of attention, lack of time, and also the prescription of lots of non-necessary chemical substances - because many doctors receive commissions from labs and from the pharmaceutical industry. In the past it was unimaginable to have a doctor, a religious or a soldier rich. No one says anything about that. It is not politically correct.

Pirates

Heavy promiscuity between large corporations and political power, in all its dimensions and instances, is reported every day by the news... sometimes covered by the well behaved title of "lobby". Such promiscuity leads millions of people to misery, seriously impoverishes the economic fabric, produces huge public debts that are automatically passed to taxpayers, and leads entire countries to bankruptcy, generating a small group of ultra-millionaires who do not participate in the market or even in society. They are mostly pirates, thieves. In fact , they became agents of commerce raiding, corsairs: bandits with official permission from governments to rob, to assault and to kill. Who says that it will be accused of conspiracy theories.

Migration

Social problems in the world are worsening rapidly. Migration fluxes from miserable countries and societies do not stop increasing. In such process, in many countries, there is a growing religious intolerance - especially by those who arrive, unlike what is generally said and what happened in the past. But if anyone unveils this, he will be accused to be xenophobic and racist. However, what happens is exactly the opposite: ancient populations are being replaced by other ones, now much more aggressive and with totalitarian spirit. If this process continues, both sides will look for radical and dictatorial leaders. The problem exists, but it is forbidden even to think about it.

Slaves

The same happens with macroeconomics. In recent years, slavery countries have competed on an equal basis with democratic ones. A competition of this nature only leads to the enrichment of interest groups and condemns to death those democratic societies perpetuating the condition of the slavery ones. The total elimination of trade barriers with countries of slave culture established a violent competitive advantage for them benefiting spurious political systems. But nothing can be done, you cannot even comment on this fact, because those who comment will immediately be condemned as xenophobic and radical, and also to be against a global integration that would save those same slave people. However, it is just the opposite: equality with slave systems makes them automatically destroy democratic systems.

Rich and Poor

Rich and poor do not pay taxes. Rich do not do so because of two basic reasons: because there is a lot of money concentrated and very few people involved - being the taxes absolute and not proportional, they must pay nothing - and also because they have money enough to hire many lawyers to find legal ways to cheat the law. The poor do not pay taxes because they are poor. So who pays taxes is the middle class - and it has being eliminated, like what happens to independent professionals and artists. It seems to be a movement of global Sovietization. Stalin or Mao Zedong were reportedly against everything that could be independent from the State. This elimination, associated with the theft declared and dedicatedly carried out by politicians, businessmen and yuppies, can only lead to disaster. But people are completely quiet. It is a taboo to talk about it.

Quotas

Several countries, such as Brazil, have usually established quotas for minorities. Quotas for Blacks, quotes to Indians or to poor people. I cannot be politically correct here saying "Afro-something" for three reasons: first because it would be hypocrisy; second because I would be obliged to make many references... like Afro-Brazilian, Afro-Chinese; Afro-Russian and I believe that we are all humans; and third because this is a text about political correctness. When the principle of quotas is applied to education, it deteriorates the educational system and recognizes competence where there is not, condemning the future of the country. The right would be to invest heavily in basic education and training of those minorities, eliminating their condition through competence. But it requires a great effort, great capacity of mobilization and organization. So, who will say that, will again be accused of being elitist and fascist.

Robin Hood reversed

Different countries around the world have gradually being controlled, through democratic means, by charismatic, populist and totalitarian-oriented leaders, but with a "left" speech, socialist - even when they are in the right wing! The difference between the action and what is said by these leaders and their followers is brutal. They claim to defend the poor, the disadvantaged; they use eloquent speeches for freedom and equality in opportunities. But, quickly and inexplicably, they become millionaires forming criminal gangs. Thus, they claim to defend the poor, but enrich and work for large corporations. Who report this type of situation, so common nowadays, is accused of being fascist and contrary to the people.

Hypocrisy

There is a widespread hypocrisy at all levels. From government to the most varied kind of institutions, from the educational system to many journalists or even to private business world and common people. Everywhere we find control - now no longer only ideological control, but also control of ideas, of free-thinking, coated with a lacquer of morality.

IMF

On September 20, 2013, the Italian television program Presa Diretta, at RAI presented a documentary about the situation of Portugal a year and a half after the entry of the IMF as the country manager. It seems that, without any exaggeration, every time the IMF intervened in an economy, the result is misery and hunger. This has happened in several countries, such as Argentina and Brazil. It would be no exception with Portugal. It is impressive - and I already said that - to have no international group of lawyers entering with a legal action against that entity at the Human Rights Court. The program focused not only Portugal, but also Germany and France, where reality is - contrarily to what is often conveyed by the media - increasingly difficult. Journalist Lisa Lotti portrayed Portugal as a country in increasing difficulty, where hunger is an irrefutable growing presence. Today, about 10% of its population is in poverty - a percentage that a few years ago would be considered impossible for a European country! We should not forget that Brazil managed to get out of an endless cycle of poverty only when Fernando Henrique Cardoso literally expelled the IMF from the country. Immediately around the world, the international financial system - even indirectly commanded by the IMF - closed the doors to Brazil, looking to strangle the country. But Cardoso's team was competent enough to face the situation.

Troika

One can argue that in fact it is not the IMF, but a troika - Russian expression curiously reminiscent from the triumvirate of the Roman Empire, that would be a declared reference to a new kind of empire - also formed by the EU and the ECB. But if we consider that these two entities seem to blindly obey to what is determined by the IMF and in nothing the current measures are distinguishable from those that over decades the IMF has applied relentlessly against various countries, all leading to misery, it seems clear that indeed, it is the IMF which is in command of Europe now.

Denounces

For decades, in a very frontal way - as in the case of John Perkins, a former IMF official - complaints have been made indicating that such entity is directly linked to the Pentagon and works only to defend the strategic interests of the United States, in a very

predatory approach, often destroying other economies. Accusations like these are extremely serious.
Or the perpetrators should be prosecuted and be in
jail, convicted of libel and slander, or it is about true
statements.

Conspiracy

At George W. Bush times, journalist Michael Moore
did in his movies a series of very serious accusations.
Apparently nothing happened. Therefore, we can
concluded that he was correct in his denounces. In
Europe the same has happened - politicians and institutions are often accused of the most varied type
of crimes. Nobody manifests and the accusations
become dead letter. In Brazil, Lula da Silva, Dilma
Rousseff or even Fernando Henrique Cardoso were
targets of very violent accusations, including murder
in the case of Lula. But nothing happened, not even
a reaction by the authorities. Nothing is denied and
nothing is clear clarified... and the accusation simply
dies because of the lack of reaction of the accused.
But there are certain denounces that should always
require an institutional reaction, because it is about
public law and its clarification is very important for
all citizens. When such doesn't happen, we apparently have evidence of criminal conspiracy by politicians and businessmen.

Germany and Italy

Surely, the most devastated country - at least in recent times - by the IMF is Greece. In fact, the Greek general government debit is the most brutal in Europe. Also, it seems to be true that European funds to EU integration were literally stolen by Greeks politicians and businessmen over the years, and the country barely has a reasonable tax structure. But it is also true that Greek economy is tiny and much of its general government debit relates to loans to purchase weapons made together German and French banks to German and French companies manufacturing weapons. Only this would be evidence of fraud. Now, the IMF, through the figure of the troika, imposes an overwhelming punitive regime against Greece, because the country is in bankruptcy and cannot afford its debts. To establish a process of killer impoverishment simply will not allow the country to pay its debts. Contrarily, it will definitively turn them impossible to be settled and will sacrifice generations. The situation in Germany and Italy after the Second World War was similar. But in 1953, the United States, Britain and France ratified the London Agreement, dramatically reduced the volume of debts of those countries, established a tremendous flexibility in their payments and represented a strong investment in the defeated countries.

Fed

Why the same thing is not done now, as it was done after World War II? Firstly because the elimination of liquidity does not happen only in Europe but also in the United States. When Fed continues its strategy of injecting money into the economy, it is only for a sector, not reaching the population as a whole - that is: it eliminates the middle class.

China

Such elimination of liquidity seems to happen because after its entry in the WTO - indeed an entry "forced" by the interests of large economic groups - China started investing, reportedly in an aggressive army, in a war navy equally aggressive, in a military space program and, in addition to the illegal annexation of Tibet - justified by the fact that much of China's drinking water come from the mountains in the Himalayas - China has expressed its clear intention of annexing islands of Vietnam - which produces oil in a jointly operation with the United States - and also to establish full control on the China Sea, now controlled by the United States. In addition, China established a true cyberwar against the United States, threatening U.S. hegemony in cyber-espionage, extended its unfair production of fake objects even to prisoners in a heavy commercial competition with the West, established an always denied policy of large currency devaluation, and expanded its influence to planetary energy corridors strategically important through indirect support to terrorist groups, as the United States did over decades.

War

The Chinese financial system, like what happens in the East in general, does not make responsible the borrower, cannot generate profit and works as a kind of political distributor of funds. A financial structure of this type - as it exists even in Japan - makes the country extremely fragile with respect to any drastic changes in the economic scenario. On the other hand, the Chinese economy - as what happened with Japan in the 1960s - is strongly dedicated to the export of cheap manufactured products. Thus, its consumer market is, par excellence, the general population of the United States and Europe - constituting nearly one billion of low cost consumers. Strangling these markets, China is crushed, as it is happening now.

Friedman

In July 2013, George Friedman said: "Following weeks of financial drama and weak economic data, the signs are now unmistakable: China is in big trouble, and the problems in its economy are deeper and even more fundamental than previously thought. (...) The Chinese are thus in a trap. If they continue aggressive lending to failing businesses, they get inflation. That increases costs and makes the Chinese less competitive in exports, which are also falling due to the recession in Europe and weakness in the United States. Allowing businesses to fail brings unemployment, a massive social and political problem. The Chinese have zigzagged from cracking down on lending by regulating informal lending and raising interbank rates to loosening restrictions on lending by removing the floor on the benchmark lending rate and by increasing lending to small- and medium-sized businesses. Both policies are problematic."

Taxes

On the other hand, the West - always dependent on the U.S. economy - has an economic model based on the war industry and came to a complicated situation. Many people refuse a strategic vision of the economy, calling it "conspiratorial." But the strategic approach has two faces: one revealing the trends established by interest groups that force and corrupt political power - an undeniable fact; and the other with the resulting trends, sometimes contradictory, of these same movements. Thus, the strategic approach is not of exclusionary nature. The process of downsizing of the global economy in the centers of consumption is evident and, according to Mark Roe, a professor at Harvard Law School, the 2008 crisis has been caused by fiscal policy, ie by heavy taxes to which institutions and populations are subjected, as I also have written since a long time.

Greece

Thus, the Greek situation seems to emerge in a new scenario. The United States and Europe will be a single market in the near future. Within this strategy, the regions under influence of China or Russia were, one by one, eliminated. Turkey is an important partner of both the United States and Europe, but it is a country with Islamic fundamentalist tendencies, at least in part of the population. Greece is Turkey's greatest enemy, already historical. The weapons purchased by Greece from German and French manufacturers, intended to establish a power of force against Turkey, to the point that Greece has created one of the most expensive armies in the world. Turkey was threatened with invasion by the Soviet Union for a long period of time, and have had the support of the United States which prevented a Soviet attack. Not only, Turkey is the beginning of one of the most important energy corridors on the planet, which extends to Afghanistan and Pakistan, and is a kind of "security gate" in relation to the radical Middle Eastern countries - and, therefore, of doubly strategic interest. In the past Turkey had to rely on the United States to prevent an invasion; now the United States and Europe look for a support from Turkey. But, it is a condition of great instability, even because Turkish politicians seem to suffer internal pressures to abandon their project of secular government as designed by Mustafa Kemal Atatürk.

Turkish aspirations

In such context, a weakening of Greece decisively attends to Turkish aspirations. One should not forget that in 2012 much of the money of Cypriots - in many cases reaching 60 % - was confiscated, reaching a large number of Russian investors. Until September 27, 2013, many banking operations in Cyprus were still suspended or reduced.

Complexity

When we look at all that we ask ourselves what is the role of the individual citizen in a world of such complexity.

Syria

If, on one hand, the United States and Europe have provided evidence that the dictatorial, monastic and perverse regime of Bashar al-Assad have used chemical weapons in Syria; on the other, Russia and China presented even apparently more compelling evidence that these same weapons have been used by the rebels, ie the United States and Europe. At this historic moment, the confrontational opposition in geo-strategic terms between two groups - the United States and Europe vs Russia and China - is evident. And when we talk about geo-strategy, we are talking about power. And when we talk about power, in any of its dimensions, instances and scales, we are talking about economy.

Democratic issues

If it is true that Barack Obama's declaration of war against Syria in 2013 was motivated by geo-strategic issues, there are other scenarios that cannot be discarded. The order of attack was suspended, evidently under pressure of Russia and China, which have in Syria their last place of influence in the Mediterranean. However, other pressures - this time of different nature - remained on the U.S. President, and they reveal, through his intemperate declarations accompanied by vacillations and contradictions, that American power, as also happens in Europe and other countries, is not exclusively determined by democratic issues.

Lies

Veja, the largest Brazilian weekly magazine announced on its cover story related to the suspension of the attack: "This time the lie did not work", referring to Obama's and John Kerry's statements classifying them as lies. Worse - Putin affirmed he had evidence according to which chemical weapons were launched by the rebels, what apparently was not denied either by the United States or by the European Union. Translation: what Putin said was that it was our tax money that cruelly murdered some fifteen hundred people, including hundreds of children! Both the CIA and the European Union assume they have actively supported the rebels with money and weapons. If Putin's statements are true, the situation is extremely serious. And... be unmasked by a personality like Putin, considered by many as a totalitarian spirit, to say the least, is not sweet.

New spending bills

Two days after Putin's announcement, apparently blocking the war on Syria, The New York Times published: "Much of the federal government will shut down as of Oct. 1 unless Congress approves new spending bills to replace expiring ones, and by mid-October, the Treasury Department will lose the borrowing authority to finance the government and pay its debts."

Great Depression

Everything seems to start in the Great Depression of 1929. Then, as now, large financial speculators produced what became popularly known as "bubbles", leading thousands of people to instantaneous misery. Suddenly, everyone wanted to redeem his assets, but they simply did not exist and the world plunged into a deep depression. In few words, people had their money in banks, the banks lend more than they had, and when people started to rescue their savings, there was no money for everyone.

Keynes

Then, the big question was: what to do? Debts were tremendously high and impossible to be paid off. The first reaction was to think in the scale of an individual: if a person was in debt and had no money, he or she should live poorly, work hard and save more. But the recipe did not work. People became even poorer, consumed less and the economy diminished more and more. So, in England, John Maynard Keynes appeared, advocating exactly the opposite: in a crisis, governments should go deeply into debt and inject money into the market through work. Thus, with the construction of infrastructures, for example, money would be distributed throughout the population, through the most varied type of activities. Since that money was a loan in its origin, it did not implicate an immediate expansion of the monetary base and therefore inflationary pressure was not too strong in the beginning. In fact, that money did not exist in the beginning, it was invisible in its origin. However, as the capital was realized, governmental debts were paid through taxation and then yes, it happened inflationary pressure. To combat inflation it was enough to keep a certain level of unemployment, obliging part of the population – the poorer – to not save. However, good part of people was not affected by this solution.

Psychology

Keynes also bet on psychology: people should believe that things were improving. In the Argentinean and Brazilian dictatorships of the 1960's and 1970s, their respective military governments constantly announced that everything was getting better in the economy and that economy was deeply psychological: people should believe and everything would be

automatically solved; who did not believe was a trai-
tor. It is difficult to understand how a so evident silly
thing counted with millions of believers! Even at the
beginning of the 21st century, several European politicians started using identical arguments, placing the
blame of the disaster on pessimistic people!

Hitler

The first person to follow closely the ideas of Keynes
was Adolf Hitler! Thus, Hitler was able to establish
a strong economy through the construction of the
famous highways and other infrastructures – what
consolidated his tyrannic power. And in his world, to
be against his orders was the same of to be immediately condemned to death. So, everything should follow the obligatory official optimism. Hitler closed the
country, preventing the money applied by the State in
infrastructures to disappear elsewhere. The formula
worked. But the more the country improved, more
State investments were needed. A vicious circle was
formed. The more the economy improved, increasing
consumption patterns, more investment was needed
to not be suddenly plunged into a new depression.
Thus came the war - an excellent tool for investment
of capital in the country with a big advantage: when
the population is convinced that it is about a just war,
there is no possible opposition. Of course, Hitler was a
criminal psychopath and simultaneously triggered the
brutal persecution against the Jews - that had nothing
to do with racial, religious or political issues: it was
pure theft, like what had happened in the Inquisition.

Eisenhower

In the context of the Depression, the economic situation in the United States in the 1930s was not good. To revert that situation, gradually, the country ceded to the ideas of Keynes and the spiral began. The Second World War made possible a large wave of investment in the country, generating a strong and sustained economic growth. This does not mean that the United States should not have fought Hitler, on the contrary! But, it shows us how all these issues are strong and, many times, contradictory. During World War II, a sort of corporation joining the armaments industry, the financial system and the army appeared - thus the Pentagon was born. Never more the country left to be involved in wars. In 1961, President Dwight D. Eisenhower made a historical alert: "We must guard against the acquisition of unwarranted influence, whether sought or unsought, by the military industrial complex. The potential for the disastrous rise of misplaced power exists and will persist. We must never let the weight of this combination endanger our liberties or democratic processes."

The value of the money

The value of the money is measured by multiplying the money that exists and flows in an economy, divided by the number of transactions in a given time period, that is, by the speed at which it circulates. It is the famous Irving Fisher's formula. As the money reduces its speed of circulation, governments decrease the interest rate, leading to a recover of speed because theoretically it is believed that low interest rates lead people to stop making financial investments and to start investing their money directly in trade, construction etc. - and because of that it is said that "there is more money in the market". With such simple trick the value of money increases. This really happens... if the costs of bureaucracy and taxes will not absorb the profits. When that happens, people start hiding the money, as they can, and there is no further investment. Then, taxes are increased and people hide even better. Because the investment of the State in the economy, with the aim of generating growth, seems to become a vicious circle, when there is no longer investment, the interest rate falls – desperately - even becoming negative, annihilating the economy in its structure and not producing results. It is crazy, but it is like that.

Interdependency

When the State's investment, even with the war industry, happens in open economies, the situation is more complicated because part of the money goes to another country. So, also because of this, more wars will be necessary. Inflationary pressure has been relatively small on the dollar - despite the tremendous expansion of its monetary base - because dollar became since a long time a currency of commodities, spread across the planet. The quantity of dollars is a secret of State and in a system of very interdependent economies, nobody can wish the death of the other.

"Armaments industry, financial corporations and army" complex

All State loans that led to a large quantity of countries in bankruptcy at the beginning of the 21st century is justified on these ideas, Keynes' ideas. When politicians and journalists declare themselves Keynesians, they are confessing their profound ignorance on economics because they ignore the spiral phenomenon. Of course, Keynes was right about many things, especially about some principles. But he could not predict the devastating disease of the industry of war, of the formation of the "armaments industry, financial corporations and army" complex, the world was not globalized, and apparently also he did not consider an essential principle: power corrupts - an inescapable truth announced by Aristotle about two thousand five and hundred years ago. It is the same to say: the human being is what he is, and economy just reflects that over thousands of years. When a government carries out loans to achieve investments in order to boost the economy, these monies pass through the hands of people without competition on one side. That is, even though there may be competition between providers of products and services, it does not exist on the side of those who make the loans and orient them to the country. So, there is an inevitable emergence of corruption - because power corrupts. When this happens, values are completely distorted, accelerating the default of the State. In the United States often corruption is known by the words "lobby" and "commission" - and it is a legal activity.

War industry

On the other hand, bureaucracy absorbs much of country's energy, erasing good part of the investment, even those emerged from the war industry.

Test

You wonder if the economy of your country is in good shape? There is a very effective way of knowing it, through a phenomenon that has happened since the Roman Empire. The value of a property has a stable relation with its rental value. In a healthy economy this ratio is around 1%. That is, the value of one month rent should be equivalent to about 1% of the value of the respective property. On the other hand, the calculation of the value of the property must obey the inverse function. This constant may vary, but not too much. Today, the rental value of a property in New York City is about 0.3% of the value of the property. After taxes and condo costs this figure drops to about 0.1%! This means that while in a healthy economy a property should be paid by their own leases in about ten years, now it is necessary a period of one hundred years to pay it! In Europe the ratio is similar. In other countries this ratio has also fallen.

Gold

Thus, in addition to the pressures at a geo-strategic level, practiced by the Pentagon, there are also strong pressures imposed by the precarious economic situation. If U.S. and European governments will not invent a new war, how could them improve the system? A system that has been supported by continuous wars for nearly seventy years? Therefore, through the structure "war industry - army - financial corporations," there is a great speculation on gold and the absence of any regulation regarding the separation between physical metal and certificates. In the 1960s, financed by the government, American companies started aggressively buying other companies in Europe. De Gaulle ordered the Bank of France to buy all gold they could, selling all reserves in dollar. It was a nightmare for the American companies and the salvation of the French ones. Now, in September 2013, in only five days, gold lose its value in 10%, without any change of the economic environment of the commodity. By contrary, in that same period the demand for physical gold increased, only certificates fluctuated as target of massive speculation. Specialized press kept silenced about that, no government or monetary authority manifested anything.

Devastating war

In a world in crisis, full of corruption, full of bureaucracy, illiquid, how to finance economy seems to be the major dilemma. Even if the present lack of liquidity in the consumption markets was generated as a mechanism of economic war against China, in parallel with a real war - in this case in Iraq and Afghanistan, impacting very specific sectors -, the key question is to know if the absence of real war in the future will not produce an even deeper crisis in the already weak economic situation of the United States and Europe, leading them to a desperate and an even more devastating war as a last resort. It seems to have happened to Hitler...

The consumer is king...

Regarding the official statements according to which both the United States and Europe are finally coming out of depression, it is apparently a sophist trick covered up by the famous fraud of GDP in an attempt to give to everything a psychological character. In fact, it's even understandable that large amounts of money are transiting between large corporations, but a country is made of people! In some sense, it is the same of what happens to gold. The movement of those large sums are disconnected from the regular citizen's daily life, but affects the accounting of the country as a whole. Try the test where you live. In recent decades giant corporations and big cartels were created, before which, countless times, political power shuts his eyes actively cooperating, in this way, with them, resulting in real thefts against entire populations in a process manifesting a cancerous growth. Then, the famous statement of the Nobel Prize Paul A. Samuelson - " The consumer is king ... " - simply disappeared .

Brutal economic asymmetry

This whole situation has designed a brutal economic asymmetry, creating two strongly independent realities: large corporations and the so-called real economy. The first exists almost independent of the latter. The volume of money moved by large corporations is higher than that moved by all the people of the world. But the accounting is just one, causing bizarre situations. Who, in the real economy, is able to pay for the overwhelming bureaucratic costs without serious risk to end in bankruptcy? The large corporations easily absorb them... and repass to you.

Thoreau

Leaving everything totally free from the State - as radical fans of Milton Friedman want – would provoke the inevitable deterioration of education, the increase of violence and the ruin of health, jeopardizing the future. People still did not realize that the economic universe operates multiple logical natures. If Thoreau is right when he says that the best State is the one that does not govern anything, he also says that "this is the State people will have when they will be ready for it," and it seems that such time has not yet arrived.

Complicated mix

In recent decades, global wealth grew vigorously, but also increased social disparities on the planet and the expansion of the monetary base in various currencies, such as the dollar and euro, grew much more than the wealth. The level of capitalization of banks is around 10% and countries, in general, are over-indebted... with economies in deep recession. It is a very complicated mix. Thus, the States would need to incur in more debt to boost their economies... relaunching the endless spiral. If they did so, they would produce more inflation and would be obliged to reduce the interest rates, which already is negative, and increase the level of unemployment, which already is at unbearable levels.

The wars

Since the World War II, the United States and, sometimes, the allies, were involved in several wars, continuously, directly against at least twenty countries. In 1947 the Cold War started, keeping the "war industry - financial system - army" complex very busy until 1991. Since 1950, the United States were involved in wars in Korea, Indochina, Cuba, Vietnam, Laos, Cambodia, Congo, Dominican Republic, Afghanistan, Grenada, Lebanon, Colombia, Libya, Iraq, Panama, Somalia, Bosnia, Sudan, Kosovo and Liberia. In 2001 the War on Terror started, involving dozens of countries. But, after the Second World War, the United States was never involved in a war against a big country. All the opponents were small. In a hyper connected world, this figure is changing now. What makes us to remind Eugene McCarthy's alert in the 1970s: "We need to know how long we will be able to support this kind of progress". Perhaps it is time to rethink it.

What we want to be

The State still has a role in society, but its role and nature have not been subject of reflection. What we want to be is the question. The idea we have, in the present state of things, is that, in general, we are condemned to incompetent, ill-prepared and uneducated leaders, working for themselves or for groups of interests, when not for criminals, without any consideration or attention to the citizen.

Syria

Everyone is attentive to what will happen to Syria in the coming days. Will be a devastating attack like those that occurred on Iraq and Libya killing millions of people and generating endless civil wars? Which country, in the current global context, can recover its economy devastated like that? Are we talking about decades or centuries? If the promised attack to Syria will happen, will also be an expansion of the conflict to Iran? What impact all that will represent on the world economy?

Attack

Firstly, it is important to focus on President Barack Obama's statement about the order to attack Syria: "I'm prepared to give that order. But having made my decision as commander in chief based on what I am convinced is our national security interests, I'm also mindful that I'm the president of the world's oldest constitutional democracy." We understand from his words that his decision is not in defense of human rights, but in defense of "our national security interests."

Chemical bombs

The controversy is over who fired chemical bombs - the despotic Assad government or the rebels, strongly supported by the United States and Europe? Putin, current spokesman of Syrian government, guarantees that it was not the Assad government. And it makes no sense that it had been it, because he was warned dozens of times that if he would had did it the country would be invaded. With a serious internal problem, whom would want things to get worse? On the other hand, a chemical attack would immediately benefit the rebels, possibly putting immediately the world at their side.

Tartus

But things are even more complex . Since 1971 the Russians have leased large port facilities in Syria, at Tartus. In 2008, Russia invested large amounts transforming those facilities into an important naval base for its war navy in the Mediterranean. Russia is the largest exporter of weapons to Syria. The region in the Mediterranean Sea off the coast of Syria, Lebanon and Israel is of great strategic importance to the energy flow, especially oil. The last place in the Mediterranean which is still under Russian influence is Syria. One by one, all countries under Russian influence were being depleted.

Corridors

Syrian relationships are even more complex. In addition to the strong relations with Russia, its great provider of weapons, the Assad government maintains close relations with China. Allegedly China would be financing Syria through overpriced oil from Iran. By its turn, Syria allegedly transfers part of the money to Taliban groups in North India - Afghanistan and Pakistan - and Maghreb, north Africa. China's presence in Africa has been very aggressive, by purchasing almost everything related to water and energy. China's interest in destabilizing North Africa is justified by the geostrategic position in relation to Europe. Regarding to northern India, it is a tremendous energy corridor, very important for the future.

Hollande

Thus, Assad has been in the opposite direction of the U.S. and European interests. But the controversy continues because public opinion in the West is of great importance, and it is unclear who fired chemical bombs. Even so, the French government of François Hollande - who ventures accelerate the trigger always present of the potential civil war between Muslims and Christians in the country - came forward with the claim that the French army will be the first to attack. There are two or three interesting elements in the assertion of the French president. Firstly, France is, in 2013, near bankruptcy, although this fact has always been vehemently denied by their governments. When the invasion of Libya happened, a very considerable amount of assets in local banks was immediately transferred to Paris, momentarily saving the country from the crisis. An attack on Syria would represent two advantages: first, it would be linked to the war industry, and today the calculation of the GDP incorporates state spending, considered as incomes; and second, because it would allow, as it happened in the attack on Libya, the U.S. government enter the war without requiring authorization from Congress.

UN

Apparently, it was that what had been planned: France attacking and the United States following. Why this has not happened? At the last moment , Barack Obama said he would seek for congressional authorization, contradicting himself. Congress should take about two to three weeks to decide. At the same time, the UN inspectors - who had previously announced that the results of the investigation would be released in four days - suddenly said that they would need two to three weeks to conduct examinations in the collected material. Of course, everything indicates that there are serious backroom negotiations between the U.S., Russia and China. So, very enlightening, François Hollande backtracked and said that, after all, he would wait for the decision of the U.S. Congress! A French government reportedly confessing his sovereign dependence on the Congress of another country.

China

All these elements also indicate that these negotiations will be related to pressure on China to change its long term geostrategic policies. China has already announced its intention to establish a large and aggressive army, to carry the war to outer space, through satellites, and to control the China Sea - unacceptable points to the United States. Therefore, the United States and Europe have established a strong policy of liquidity shortage in those who are the only true consumer markets in the world, pressing China.

Stalin

Thus, if there will be an attack on Syria, it will not target only a country, but also Iran, Russia, China and the northern India region. Local populations will certainly be taken as predictable collateral damage without any importance beyond statistics, seeming to assume as true the famous and hated Stalin's claim according to which: "One death is a tragedy, a million deaths is a statistic data."

Strategic decisions

Other countries took immediate strategic decisions. A few days before the announcement of President Obama, the Federal Reserve announced a sudden change in the process of capital injection into the economy, reducing the expansion of the monetary base and reversing the inflationary trend. Brazil, for example, launched currency swaps – species of bonds operating in different currencies. So, one buys a paper with a currency and receives its value when trading in other currency, meaning that the country "sold" reserves of foreign currency. But, in a situation of serious war involving great powers, these papers can simply no longer be paid, reversing the sale made previously. Thus, the country sells, but does not sell.

Fundamental

The fundamental question is not whether the dictator Assad should or should not be removed, if the Syrian people should or should not be helped. It is obvious that dictatorships are not acceptable. The essential point is that, to all appearances, this is not anything related to a people, the persons, to human beings, but yes to planetary economic conflicts involving worldwide geostrategic movements. And another issue, as important as that one, is to know about what democracy is based on. Is there one single example of democratic system without literature in the world – in any epoch? Never!

Nobel Prize

Even in the case of a Nobel Peace Prize, could the president be condemned for his decision? Would he have another alternative? The problem is that the current politicians are still politicians of the nineteenth century. A chain of leaders, obeying to the interests of large economic groups, who think as people thought more than a hundred years ago. But, one could expect that the leader of the greatest country in the world should contribute with a contemporary thought. While the nineteenth century, strongly literary, established the principles of desegregation and conflict – because of it Marx took work as exploration and not as collaboration - technologies of the 21st century are strongly integrative. But how to be integrator when other parts are not? Perhaps for the first time in a long time, the collective intelligence of the streets will give some answer.

Newspapers

In recent days newspapers from all over the world have published disconcerting news, to say the least. And the lack of public reaction to them is even more disconcerting, also to say the least. I choose, almost randomly, four of them.

Real estate

In August 6 2013, The New York Times published an interesting article on the public financing of real estate in the United States: "In the seven years since the housing market started to fall apart, politicians of both parties have promised repeatedly to build a better system for financing the American dream of owning a home. There is little sign of progress. (...) The federal government guaranteed about 87 percent of new mortgage loans last year, through Fannie Mae and Freddie Mac and the Federal Housing Administration, effectively setting the terms and providing the money for nine out of 10 home purchases and refinanced loans. (…) The president praised a bipartisan Senate effort to replace Fannie and Freddie with a system that would charge lenders for explicit government guarantees of some mortgage loans". Then, the journalist of The New York Times added: "Americans like cheap mortgage loans and it is hard to preserve the benefits without the costs of the current system." But what this means? Is there any other people in the world that dislikes cheap mortgages? So, should we understand from the article that the Americans are guilty because they like cheap mortgage loans and this negatively affects their benefits? Why is the government subsiding the real estate market? Wouldn't be the problem located in the lack of liquidity generated by a gradual transformation from an economy of savings to an economy of debit? Not a single word about that. It seems that, accordingly to the article, the American people is the guilty. Simply unbelievable!

IMF

The other news, published in several newspapers on August 2, 2013, informed the new orientation of the IMF, headed by Mrs. Christine Lagarde, to Spain: to reduce all salaries by 10% and reducing social benefits by 1.7 %. First of all, everyone knows that the problem of insolubility of the Mediterranean countries is due to a complex combination of terrible factors: financial mafias associated with political mafias that indebted countries beyond what would be acceptable in democratic regimes; massive theft by public officials, politicians, banks, companies and other entities; rapid growth of bureaucracy, and huge increase of taxes - which caused the debt to grow even more. But shouldn't the economic system be balanced by itself? - or should it be conducted by the State, like what happened in the Soviet regime? The values indicated by the IMF in nothing will change the situation of these countries if those elements will not be changed. It is impossible the IMF not know about that. I never understood why groups of lawyers have never filed lawsuits against that entity in the Court of Human Rights in The Hague.

Money laundering

On August 7, 2013, the award-winning business and energy journalist Anthony Harrington published an interesting article about U.S.'s steps in the battle against money laundering. He writes: "The global financial crisis has brought a huge windfall for organized crime networks. Banks have profited handsomely from terrorists and drug lords, channelling billions of dollars through the U.S. financial system, while the European debt crisis has cemented the grip of the mafia on underground economies in peripheral eurozone countries like Italy and Spain. European authorities are now taking action against the staggering web of corruption – but is it too late?." But, if the crimes are public, as he courageously says, why nothing was ever made to stop them? Which are the beneficiary banks, entities and persons? He continues: "Part of the problem the Basel Committee, and regulators in general face, is that money, in the sort of quantities that we are talking about, has a hugely corrosive power. It has the capacity to subvert politicians, police and regulators alike, all of whom are on salaries that look minuscule by comparison with the bribes that could be on offer." This makes us to conclude that we are dominated by bandits, in all levels of society!

Surveillance

Today, August 9, 2013, The New York Times published an article about Mr. Obama and the controversial NSA's technologies of surveillance. According to the newspaper, Mr. Obama said that "It's right to ask questions about surveillance, particularly as technology is reshaping every aspect of our lives. (…) It's not enough for me, as president, to have confidence in these programs. The American people need to have confidence in them as well." But! It is not a question of confidence! It is a question of defense of a Rule of Law. It is not a personal question, it is not about marketing – it is a question of values.

Two dimensions

Observe, look at your side. When I see renowned economists brandishing empty abstractions, I wonder where their actual competence is. Macro and micro-economy, although are two different scales - and therefore two different universes - are always inextricably linked. One is impossible without the other: they are communicating vessels in different dimensions.

Real life

Look at real life, at what happens in your life and near you. Banks no longer have the social function that was born in the Middle Ages. With negative interest rates, money lost part of its value. The value of money exists both in consumption and in savings. This second value simply ceased to exist.

Savings in Roman Empire

Savings finished. Worldwide, real estate leases simply finished as a form of savings. High taxes, the cost of bureaucracy and the illiquidity devastated this ancient form of saving, which was common even in the Roman Empire.

ECB

Banks now operate negative interest rates. On the first day of August 2013, Mario Draghi, ECB president, announced that interest rates will remain negative for a long time. Japan did exactly that and plunged its economy into a recession that has dragged on for nearly twenty years! It is an economic policy that devastates countries. Who benefits from this? States because they can fund themselves with what would be the savings of their populations. With that, economy suffers terribly because there is a rapid drying up of liquidity. On the other hand, prevented of compensating the money that is deposited by their clients, banks became institutions exclusively devoted to speculation.

High-frequency trading

The financial systems became so oriented to speculation that many of the people involved in them argue that is not possible to survive without fraud. A clear example is the so-called high-frequency trading, which is about the use of sophisticated technology and computer algorithms to fast trade securities, making financial movements in seconds or fractions of a second. The frauds in high frequency trade are so evident that, despite be a recent novelty, having started only in 1999, it already has an inventory of the most used tools of trickery. The three more used are saturation, noise and aggression. In saturation, the system simply clogs the business structure with ghost orders. In noise, orders are sent and cancelled in milliseconds, confusing the entire system. Aggression is when a huge quantity of orders flow is made in one and other direction, provoking huge depreciation of a commodity, like gold for example.

Authority

No authority, no government, no institution, no central bank, no federal reserve condemn those spoofs. But if you steal someone, even in few dollars, you will go to jail.

Paralyzing

Thus, the world is stopping, day after day more and more paralyzed. But the governments say that everything is getting better! When such a denial is no longer possible, they say that the guilty is of the people not paying taxes and create waves of fiscal terror, that paralyze even more the economy.

Failure as a thinking animal

The only justifiable question is about if it is a gen-eralized stupidity or if all this is made according to geo-strategy, that is to say: if it is a new kind of war. But following the quality of the politicians, that cre-ate laws to protect themselves, the most probable is that we are dealing with both realities. This reminds me of John Steinbeck when he said that "all war is a symptom of human's failure as a thinking animal." And Aeschylus: "In war, truth is the first casualty."

Two reasons

A quick approach on the world now reveals startling facts for two reasons: because of their frightening radicalism and because of the generalized numbness of people.

Europe

Europe crushes its southern countries and establishes a growing bureaucracy, seeming to aspire to a future Soviet model. Bureaucracy is an excellent humus for corruption. The Southern European States are massacred by their corrupted politicians associated to also corrupted businessmen (many times from the north), by the big financial systems, big corporations, and by a growing debt that often seems to be odious. In all this situation there is no judgment, no punishment and no responsibility.

US

The United States gave up, apparently permanently, of the basic pilars of democracy: there is no longer habeas corpus, the division of powers is weakened, and monetary policy benefits in clear way large corporations - in fact, like what also happens in Europe. Wars are made to benefit economic groups and so on. No one is judged!

Law

In both continents, privacy stopped being something significant. Instead, the intelligence services at all levels are increasingly active, remembering, with increasing intensity, the figure of Big Brother created by George Orwell. The American omnipotence in Europe is such that Washington seemed to have ordered the immediate closure of airspace to the airplane of the president of Bolivia, who would be transporting a former CIA agent. Incidentally, the right to political refuge that such former agent has, an international law that is recognized by the United Nations, is simply denied by the United States - as if it was telling to the world: we are above the law

Corruption

In both continents, big corporations and large financial systems seem to have corrupted politicians of all kinds, and destroying large sectors of the population.

Decay

Education standards are lower and lower. Pharmaceutical industry has increasingly extraordinary profits. All saving mechanisms have been eliminated. Copyrights have gradually being eliminated. Control and surveillance of people have being increasingly overwhelming. Taxes go up dramatically and the value of labor decreases in equal proportion. Everything becomes superficial and immediate, continuous and low-quality consumption in short cycles.

Other places

If we look at other places of our planet, the situation will not be much different. The declared goal of the Chinese government in early 2012 for the following five years was to strength the control on its population. In Brazil, popular movements denounce the complicity, if not direct involvement, of the government in all sorts of crimes. Africa remains destroyed. Drug trafficking seems to be always stronger worldwide.

Sleeping-walkers

What is the result of all this? Simply nothing. People seem to be narcotized, like sleeping-walkers. Everyone seems to be satisfied with a seemingly low cost gilded prison.

Orwell

Facts that remind us of George Orwell when he said: In a time of universal deceit - telling the truth is a revolutionary act.

Market economy

What are the essentials of what we call "market economy"? What we could identify as its essential elements? The so-called market economy may suffer a heavier or lighter interventionism from the respective State, but there are limits. Even in general terms, those limits are defined by two major areas: the first one formed by health, education and culture, which can be more freely subsidized by the states, because they belong to a logical universe which is different of that one of the called "production and trade", the second area. It is curious to observe how great part of Americans simply ignore such a so primary fact, and how Europeans seem to happily run at this ignorance.

Material and immaterial dimensions of things

Recognized such a division, we start noticing where the political world should never enter: in the immaterial dimension of the first area – in sectors of health, education and culture; and in the material dimension of the second major area: the sectors of production and trade. That is, no power has the right to intervene in scientific discovery, education and art. What we see as probable exceptions, as shown in the controversies surrounding genetics or the production of weapons, would normally be better regulated by civil society.

Relations

On the other hand, the State has no right to intervene in the material universe of production and trade, but it can establish an important role in relation to its intangible dimension, regulating copyright, for example, checking for crimes like cartels, dumping etc.. When this happens, the State operates on relationships and not on the material dimension of things.

Aristotle

But within this universe, we have other essential conditions a market economy. The rule of Law is one of its sacred pillars. Without it, it is impossible market economy to exist. For the Rule of Law, isonomy - equality of all in face of Law - is essential. Aristotle said: "It is more proper that law should govern than any one of the citizens: upon the same principle, if it is advantageous to place the supreme power in some particular persons, they should be appointed to be only guardians, and the servants of the laws."

Courts

But for the Law to work, courts need to work well. A society dominated by money, where the purchase of more expensive attorney and lawyers services can mean victory in the bar of the courts, is not a free society, it doesn't operate under the Rule of Law and cannot have a real market economy.

Freedom

Another fundamental principle for a market economy is freedom. Where there is no freedom, no free market is possible. Freedom - and here I am saying about the concept of "negative freedom" - is the responsibility of each one of us to determine our own limits. When the State manipulates the nation through abusive taxes, unjustifiable and unacceptable debts, so many times fruit of indecorous lobbies, but also even through tax persecution - the so-called "fiscal terrorism" - no free market can exist.

Prevention

This freedom brings in itself an essential condition: everyone is free to do whatever he or she want, the State can only punish a posteriori, after the crime is committed. When the State acts preventively, the conditions for the existence of a free market disappear.

Privacy

But freedom also implies privacy: that I know that only I know what will be my next step. If we have watched our phones, our letters opened, we penetrate the darkness of totalitarianism and the market conditions die.

Stability

Another condition is of great importance to legal stability. Laws should be stable, must remain in their form for decades, so that a free market can be established. When laws change every week, the end is near - as we learnt from the ancient Rome.

Lie

For all these conditions can be met, there can be no manipulation of the truth, economic indices can not be defrauded. There is no acceptable justification for the lie. Information should be free, but must also comply with privacy principles, if applicable.

The State

Thus, no State can allow, in the labyrinths of their corridors, the emergence of cartels or monopolies, under any pretext.

Free Courts

But once again fell into an essential need: the courts must always be free and independent. At the moment there is corruption of the magistrate, or the slowness of legal proceedings benefit criminal conduct, free market can never exist.

Neocapitalism

Sometimes, in several countries, I hear political groups say they blame the global economic disaster for something called "neocapitalism" - without being able to explain what it actually is. But! It this is not a "new capitalism", as the expression "neocapitalism" indicates, but yes a "new economic fascism." Therefore, the dictator Benito Mussolini said: "Fascism should rightly be called Corporatism, as it is the merger of corporate and government power."

Strange drop

Gold just knew a precipitous and strange drop in its value of reference. Its value was profoundly depreciated. The only possible official justification is possibly based on a worldwide depressed economic activity. But neither the governments say that, neither it is a justifiable fact in proportional terms to the crisis.

Contradictory

In February, immediately before the first major devaluation of the metal of the last times, China had announced an annual increase of 9.35% on the purchase of gold. But even thus, the value of gold fell. Contradictory data.

Predictions

The Economist Intelligence Unit predicted that the

global consumption of gold would fall 4.7% in 2013, after a fall of 6.2% in 2012, and that it would be a reverse trend in 2014. First of all, such a forecast indicates that the moments of great increase of gold price coincides with the decrease of its consumption! But... if we are working accordingly to market laws it should be exactly the opposite! Then the EIU was wrong again about 2013 – gold fell around 30% in the first semester of 2013, not 4.7%! One could risk arguing that it was about a retarded reaction to the decrease of consumption. But... a retarded reaction of two years in our hyper connected world?! On the other hand, the UBS bank predicts now a fall to 1,000 dollars an ounce in the next months. If the UBS forecasts are correct, the Economist Intelligence Unit's experts will be even more dramatically wrong.

More contradictions

In the last quarter of 2012, India had announced an annual growth of 35% in acquisition of gold. According to the World Bureau of Metal Statistics the world production of gold rose 7.8% in 2010, when paradoxically it was a greater appreciation of metal, and fell in 2011 and 2012, when – again paradoxically - the production of the metal maintained a certain balance, and experienced a dramatic decline in early 2013. Few months ago Germany requested 321 tonnes of its physical gold repatriated back out of the US. The same happened some months before with Venezuela, with 200-plus tonnes. The US repatriated Venezuela's gold, but promised to send Germany's gold only in seven years! These data are simply contradictory. Why the US repatriated gold to Venezuela and not to Germany? Some critics say that it would be about a control on the flux of the metal.

Pressure

The pessimistic forecast of the World Bureau of Metal Statistics indicates that the value of gold will be at $1,350 an ounce in 2015. The Swiss bank Credit Suisse believes that the world economy will improve in the second half of 2013 and that, therefore, it will be less demand for gold! Anyway, it should be the opposite in all senses. After all, no serious economist believes in such an improvement of the world economy in the second semester of 2013. Moreover, historically, any improvement of the world economy has always being accompanied by a maintenance of the value of the metal or its appreciation. On the other hand, it seems to exist a continuing pressure of global inflation, which always historically led to an appreciation of gold. In apparent paradox, some economists indicate that the devaluation of gold reveals rather a deflationary pressure! Inflation or deflation, historically, both led to an appreciation of gold.

Gold Act

It is important to remind the Gold Act of 1933, or more specifically the Executive Order 6102 of April 5 1933, when the American government requested all people's gold, physical and in certificates, by May 1, 1933. Then, all gold was retired even from the private boxes in the banks. After that, when a substantial quantity of gold were already in power of the authorities, government devaluated dollar from 20.67 to 35.00 per ounce through the Gold Reserve Act of January 31, 1934. Now, it is possible that a new currency emerges, having gold and other metals in its composition. It is not impossible to have a new requisition of gold from American, European and other governments.

Tricks

The great rise of gold after 2005 coincides with the beginning of an intense expansion of the monetary basis in 2003 in both the United States and Europe. This expansion is sometimes disguised in form of credit. That is, it is made in form of injection of liquidity through the increase of debt. This means that with such strategy there is no nominal expansion of money, at least in accounting terms, but only increase of debt. But the market is sensitive to this tricks and can not be fooled for a long time.

Certificates

The information about gold consumption in the last months reveals two interesting facts - first, that the fall in demand is not proportional to the fall of the value of the metal, which is much higher. Second, that the big drop occurs almost exclusively in gold certificates!

Curve

If we observe the behavior of gold since the year 1900 we will see that there is implicitly a logarithmic curve upward. Such line shows an upward trend of recovery in the medium and long term.

General data

The growth of equities has been minimal; the value of the US GDP growth is possibly masked by the government; the inflation rate has been masked by selection criteria of products in the basket and respective subsidies; unemployment has also being questionable; the value of gold is very low; interestingly, the value of oil remains high; and the American ten-year bonds pay a fraction of the inflation!

Manipulation

Will be all that about market manipulation? It is interesting to have in mind the gold fall on April 12, 2013. In just few minutes there was a massive sale of gold (certificates) on the market. A huge movement during the night, selling simultaneously a huge quantity of gold (in certificates). Very interestingly no authority in any country investigated the case.

This is clear evidence of manipulation. On the other hand, the pressures for the maintenance of the value of the metal continue.

Expansion

Now, let's consider the options of a non-speculator (as it is our case). Simply, they no longer exist. The real estate market is collapsed, buried under direct or indirect taxes and other costs. The financial market only offers corrosion or high risk. Moreover, even when the risk in financial market is apparently low, the real trends do no permit low risk. The political and economic trends for the second half of 2013, for example, are terrible – just have in mind Brazil, it represents a trend that promises to expand to other countries in the coming months. The expansion of the monetary base, euphemistically called "quantitative easing" by the US governments, remains intensely applied.

More certificates

Exactly when there is a greater expansion of the the monetary basis the value of gold falls brutally?! This is even more striking when we consider the fact that the drop does not justify the reduction of demand, which happened almost exclusively in certificates. It makes no sense, reinforcing the thesis of manipulation.

Conditions

Thus, the present conditions are maintained: no option for investment; economics is still (and will be) extremely uncertain eliminating the migration of values in gold for the productive system; interest rates continue negative, the real estate industry is greatly affected - all these factors imply a pressure on gold as safe haven. On the other hand, countries like China and India did not reduced significantly their positions as buyers; the industrial sector also did not reduce dramatically the consumption of the metal; there already are countries where there is no more physical gold available; the industrial production of gold is much smaller than the growth of the world economy, and its reserves are stable – all these factors imply a pressure for recovery, appreciation or at least for the maintenance of the value of gold.

Concentration

What can happen? Giving that there is clear evidence of manipulation, the value of gold may fall further. One of the tricks for speculation – as I pointed several months ago – is the intensive operation on certificates market, which falsely affects the value of physical gold. If that happens, a maintenance of the low values can be generated over the next months forcing the migration of reserves that are now held by small investors, creating a strong concentration, like a singularity of gold in governments and large banks.

Panic

But there are two important general indicators: first, the tendency to medium-term recovery in real value. Secondly, the fact that we are in a so volatile universe that during this period serious jumps can occur: a scenario even more exciting for speculators. In this situation, for those who are not speculating, for the called conservative savers, the best is to wait and see, never to be in panic.

Mathematics

Bank forecasts are generated by mathematical models. Thus, the trends rendered by them are established through the observation of evolution according to historical data with decreasing importance. They do not point fast course changes – only if they are recurrent in historical terms. At the end of 2012 the UBS forecasts, for example, pointed to a gold value of about $ 1,850 an ounce. Only six months later, their prediction value fell to about $ 1,000. The trend change occurred due to the change of the data already happened, i.e., a posteriori.

Deflation

But there is also another phenomenon: what happens

when the value of all things like real estate, gold, and other commodities fall? The response is: deflation. Interestingly, eleven years ago, in 2012, Ben Bernanke said: "The sources of deflation are not a mystery. Deflation is in almost all cases a side effect of a collapse of aggregate demand - a drop in spending so severe that producers must cut prices on an ongoing basis in order to find buyers. Likewise, the economic effects of a deflationary episode, for the most part, are similar to those of any other sharp decline in aggregate spending - namely, recession, rising unemployment, and financial stress." It is as if he was describing the world today.

Bernanke 2

That same year, Ben Bernanke said that "Sustained deflation can be highly destructive to a modern economy and should be strongly resisted. Fortunately, for the foreseeable future, the chances of a serious deflation in the United States appear remote indeed, in large part because of our economy's underlying strengths but also because of the determination of the Federal Reserve and other U.S. policymakers to act preemptively against deflationary pressures." But the American economy only suffered since then and I do not think that the economic policy has being successful - at least in terms of immediate people's objectives. Perhaps it makes sense under less clear and hidden objectives.

Rickards

What happens to gold when we have deflation? It gains in value. Few days ago, Jim Rickards, working at Tangent Capital, said a: "The problem is when central banks fear deflation more than anything, they try everything to defeat it, so, you know, currency wars, money printing, zero-interest-rate policy, forward guidance, twist. They do everything they can. When they can't win the battle against deflation, they devalue the currency against gold 'cause gold's the only thing that can't fight back". And he's right.

Two scenarios

Now imagine to mix two scenarios: a deep framework of speculation operated by large institutions, associated to government; and deflation... Thus, the situation becomes even more complicated and uncertain. In Brazil, there is a shadow of dictatorship and civil war manifesting through intense popular protests and the reactions of the government. The same can happen soon in Europe and the US. The credibility of governments is increasingly low, almost throughout the world.

Thomas Jefferson

Ok. If we are dealing with speculators, we need to imagine how they think. They want money. So, if all the manifested manipulations are part of a huge process of speculation – we had several examples like that in the last few years – we can wait for a big increase of gold value in the next months. However, if we will have, in some way, something like a new Gold Act... the future is uncertain. Banks pay nothing for your money, taxes are devastating, corruption is a little everywhere, and we can imagine if the governments will usurp gold!

In one or other way, up to where we already arrived, all that has happened under the mandate of more and more powerful governments, even if so many times they do nothing regarding so important questions. What brings to my mind Thomas Jefferson when he said that "my reading of history convinces me that most bad government results from too much government."

Brazil

Suddenly, Brazil started a popular revolt this week. A country of two hundred million inhabitants is revolted from north to south. Hundreds of thousands, if not millions, of people in the streets. Perhaps it is about a true revolution - if such is still possible in the 21st century. What these people are asking for? Four simple things: fighting corruption, supporting education, health and security. It is the right of any people aspire to such basic conditions. What has happened in recent years in Brazil?

Education

Brazilian government invests six times less in education than the US government. OECD analyzed 35 countries and Brazil is in antepenultimate position, behind countries like Chile, Argentina and Mexico. From its two hundred million inhabitants just six and a half million get to university. Graduation has been considered, both in Europe, South Korea, Japan or the United States as "the most basic education." To get an idea of how Brazil is underdeveloped in terms of education, more than 60% of South Korean population enroll in a university. Brazilian population, provided with means such as the Internet, know that. In July 2012 the Brazilian Finance Minister Guido Mantega said that if the goals of investment of 10% of GDP in education were met, Brazil would enter in bankruptcy! PISA Program for International Student Assessment examinations in 2009 revealed that the Brazilian education is in 53rd place among 65 countries, behind Trinidad and Tobago! But, this is perfectly consistent with the former president, Lula da Silva, who argued, in 2009, that it is not necessary to study to be intelligent or to reach success. He himself proudly declared in several occasions to have never studied.

Corruption

Never, in its entire history, the country had so overwhelming corruption as today. According to Transparency International, Brazil is one of the most corrupt countries in the world. Its reports state that "Scandals involving cabinet ministers and business leaders in 2012 have also highlighted corruption allegations in public procurement. Corruption vulnerability is only heightened by the government's US$66 billion road project and millions more being funneled to produce two of the world's largest gaming events: the 2014 World Cup and 2016 Olympics." The soccer World Cup in Japan in 2002 cost $16 billion; the world cup in Germany cost $6 billion in 2006; and the South African cup consumed 8 billion in 2010 - together, the three events cost $30 billion. Just the Brazilian Cup and Olympic Games will cost nearly $70 billion, while all the World Cups, of all times, together, cost about 75 billion dollars. Translation: all the money generated by these events are already committed to companies considered trustful by the government.

Violence

Brazil is now one of the twenty most violent countries in the world. Amnesty International denounces that in addition to the high number of violent crimes, the Brazilian government makes widespread use of torture. The report also informs that in 2012 violent crimes and murders increased "dramatically" in the city of São Paulo. Not only in the big cities, Brazilians feel unsafe even to walk in the streets!

Health

The public health situation in Brazil is so outrageously bad that President Dilma Rousseff announced, in response to the revolted people, that she would "immediately bring thousands of doctors from abroad", specifically from Cuba. In fact, Cuba is a country with a lot of doctors, but unfortunately they are amongst the most back-warded in the world - even in Brazil only 5% of them are able to have a revalidation of their diplomas. The essential question is: can a government that led a country to this situation continue governing? Not to say that hiring Cuban doctors reminds the African techniques, especially in Angola, to control population in the 1970s.

Cardoso

All those promises of campaign were not fulfilled either by the Lula government, either by the government of Dilma. Some people believe that Lula was responsible for the democratization and modernization of Brazil - but this is a huge mistake. Lula sold such image, with aggressive and expensive marketing - just the feature movie of propaganda, Lula Son of the People, launched in 2010 was the most expensive in the Brazilian history of cinema, and it was paid by constructors with active contracts with the government. Who made the reforms that transformed Brazil was Fernando Henrique Cardoso, brilliant sociologist. His economic measures changed Brazil's face.

Barbosa

Lula is a man who claims to be ignorant but honest. Years ago, a supporter of Lula asked me if such a fact was not a great thing for the country – to have for president a miserable ignorant, but honest person. Then I replied saying that honesty should be a sine qua non condition for anyone who aims a government function and, furthermore, he or her should always be very competent, ie he or she should never be ignorant. Apart from ignorance, Lula seems also to have been involved in crimes like the murder of a politician in São Paulo State, Celso Daniel. Eight witnesses were mysteriously murdered, without a shadow of the assassins. No one was convicted. Now, Lula was intimately related to the convicted criminals of the largest corruption case in the history of the country, called Mensalao. Result: although convicted in the Supreme Court, those criminals are free and continue working as deputies in the national congress! To make matters worse: they are working on new laws against the judiciary that condemned them! The judge Joaquim Barbosa, who sentenced them, became a national hero.

PEC 37

Given the difficult situation that emerged from the condemnation of the partners of Lula and Dilma, in the most devastating case of corruption in the history of the country, the administration of Dilma Rousseff drew a crude solution: eliminate the judiciary. How? The present Brazilian government drawn up a proposed constitutional amendment with number 37/2011, simply abbreviated as PEC 37. It is a project which aims to limit the power of criminal investigation, removing the public prosecutors! - who condemned the partners of Lula and Dilma. If this law is approved, the public prosecutors will not be able to investigate politicians in Brazil! It is very comprehensible that people are angry. There are even rumors that the Brazilian secret police is identifying and classifying good part of the protesters, also on the social networks - a fact that, if true, would transform it into a new political police. And it is an irony of history, to say the least, that a president who was a confessed terrorist attacks protesters.

US

Do you think all this serious? But, in a sense, this also happens in the United States. In the administration George W. Bush, Dick Cheney joined from the oil services megacompany Halliburton; Karl Rove, chief political strategist, had been chief political strategist at Philip Morris between 1991 and 1996; Mitchel Daniels, head of the White House Office of Management and Budget, was vice president of the chemical empire Eli Lilly; the Secretary of Treasure, Paul O'Neill, came from the giant aluminum company Alcoa; and Condoleezza Rice, Secretary of State, came from Chevron.

Halliburton

It is interesting to read a fragment of the Wikipedia article about Halliburton, collected today: Halliburton has become the object of several controversies involving the 2003 Iraq War and the company's ties to former U.S. Vice President Dick Cheney. Cheney retired from the company during the 2000 U.S. presidential election campaign with a severance package worth $36 million. As of 2004, he had received $398,548 in deferred compensation from Halliburton while Vice President. Cheney was chairman and CEO of Halliburton Company from 1995 to 2000 and has received stock options from Halliburton. In the run-up to the Iraq war, Halliburton was awarded a $7 billion contract for which 'unusually' only Halliburton was allowed to bid. Bunnatine Greenhouse, a civil servant with 20 years of contracting experience, had complained to Army officials on numerous occasions that Halliburton had been unlawfully receiving special treatment for work in Iraq, Kuwait and the Balkans. Criminal investigations were opened by the U.S. Justice Department, the Federal Bureau of Investigation (FBI) and the Pentagon's inspector general. In one of Greenhouse's claims, she said that military auditors caught Halliburton overcharging the Pentagon for fuel deliveries into Iraq. She also complained that Defense Secretary Donald Rumsfeld's office took control of every aspect of Halliburton's $7 billion Iraqi oil/infrastructure contract. After her testimony, Greenhouse was demoted for poor performance. Greenhouse's attorney, Michael Kohn, stated in The New York Times that 'she is being demoted because of her strict adherence to procurement requirements and the Army's preference to sidestep them when it suits their needs'."

Manipulation

Countless articles argue that Tony Blair lied about Iraq war. Many denounces showed the evident conflict of interests of Mr. Berlusconi's position as Italian prime minister. Spain, Portugal, and France are full of scandals, among many other countries – with a single common result: nothing. No one was convicted, no one is in prison. Billions of dollars were magically "lost", and no one knows anything about. Gold manipulation, frauds of all kinds, transformation of the banks in tools for robbery, scandalous financial systems, corruption everywhere, low level of education and health. It is perfectly comprehensible that soon or later people get furious.

Beuys

Shortly before his death, the famous German artist Joseph Beuys said, in 1985, that "every individual shall become a co-author with the awareness that he is sovereign and that he should give to suffrage fair conceptions and fair economic laws which should govern the future." But! Isn't this exactly what the Brazilian people proposes through the protests? It will not be a surprise if this overwhelming movement invade both the United States and Europe. It is a generational change.

Three outcomes

Few outcomes appear: either people who work in the administration of countries become more honest; or it will be a widespread civil war; or the States gradually establish totalitarian governments where silent terror will reign, controlling everything and everyone through telecommunication systems.

Planetary domination

We have heard almost throughout most of the twentieth century, presidents and statesmen declaring a "new world order". From Woodrow Wilson and Winston Churchill to George Bush (father and son) to Barak Obama, directly or indirectly. From Freemasons, to Jews, to the communism, nazism and even to the invasion of extraterrestrial - almost everything has been speculated about the formation of planetary domination by a small group of people... or aliens. And interestingly, even though these historical references, recent American presidents have consistently repeated speeches in defense of a "new world order".

The future

Everything is in continuous transformation and, forgetting the conspiratorial character of the phrase "new world order", the global order has been permanently in transformation in apparent acceleration. When we hear the fervent advocacy of a system of annulment of privacy, of heavy surveillance mechanisms, espionage and control of all people, in order to prevent terrorist attacks (assuming Machiavelli's maximum according to which the ends justify the means), as defended by the American President - a lawyer! - we all get very concerned about a "new world order", and about what such statement really means.

Privacy

The computer scientist Jaron Lanier said: "Facebook says, 'Privacy is theft,' because they're selling your lack of privacy to the advertisers who might show up one day." The recent announcement that the U.S. government seems to have no barriers in its determination to invade the privacy of citizens and foreigns, angered part of the world, especially in Europe. The Germans have even classified the US government determination - "the means justify the ends" - as typical measures of the Stasi, the former communist political police, responsible for killing thousands of people. But a new poll by the Washington-Post newspaper shows that "a large majority of Americans say the federal government should focus on investigating possible terrorist threats even if personal privacy is compromised, and most support the blanket tracking of telephone records in an effort to uncover terrorist activity." What seems to be normal for the American mentality, seems to be deeply unusual for Europeans.

Mega free trade agreement

In Feb 12, 2013, president Obama announced a mega free trade agreement between Europe and the United States. There is a logic behind it, and its scale shows that it is not a new idea, but something that surely has been worked behind curtains over the last several years. Immediately, Chancellor Angela Merkel declared that such an agreement is "by far our most important project for the future." But Christoph Pauly and Christoph Schult, journalists from the respected German magazine Der Spiegel, published an article, days after Obama's announcement, saying: "it appears that not everyone in Europe agrees" with Canceller Merkel. And they points to some differences between American and European mentalities: "US companies like Facebook and Google see European data privacy as a potential threat to their billions in profits. (…) What do we want to eat? How are our personal data treated in the Internet? In recent years, very different traditions have developed in the United States and Europe in this regard, creating considerable potential for conflict. For instance, there are much greater restrictions on the sale of genetically modified food products in Europe, while most Americans have no problem with such products, as long as they are cheap and look good. (…) The American farm lobby has long fought against European trade barriers for genetically modified potatoes and hormone-treated beef. Now the free trade treaty will provide them with considerable leverage for cracking the European front."

Chinese market

What would be the solution? Simply enter and start transforming Europe, which has been less profitable than the American market. And the first step would simply be starting the free trade locking alternatives through bureaucratic and political tools. Yesterday, the Swiss newspaper Le Temps published an article about the indignation of the filmmaker Ursula Meier, saying that the "European Union should not to mislead the precise moment when the Commission must adopt the final negotiating mandate of the agreement free trade Europe – USA. This Friday, June 14, Europe may be entering a new era in which the political abdicates to face the single market logic by sacrificing one of its most valuable assets: the culture."

Huge new market

And why Europe would do that? Because the free trade agreement will create a gigantic market with more than one billion consumers. Almost as big as the Chinese market, but much richer. The United States have about three hundred million people and Europe has more than seven hundred million. About 50% of the European population speaks English. The clumsy expansion of Europe had, after all, a good strategic reason: the creation of a huge new market.

Formatting

What would be the best format for such a market? A simple answer: lots of low quality and big quantity consumers. But, the European tradition is exactly the opposite. So, to change it is necessary a strong decrease of liquidity, impoverishing people and concentrating power of consumption on credit, which is easier controlled. Today, June 14, 2013, many people in Europe are deeply worried with the future of their lives, fearing a rapid transformation of their countries into places without art, culture, books, or authentic cooking – countries transformed into places dominated by industrial logic. Many Europeans think that the majority of Americans are unaware of this phenomena. We, here in the United States, often believe that Europeans are not objective, that they are poorly organized and, especially in southern countries, that they are the only ones to blame for the situation in which they find themselves.

Irony

Irony of history, Vladimir Lenin said "The way to crush the bourgeoisie is to grind them between the millstones of taxation and inflation." Having a continent transformed in bourgeoisie, now it seems that it is the IMF, the ECB and the UE, together with the US, to follow to Lenin's lessons.

Perkins

Why the IMF - an organization based in Washington - is lending money to Europe and controlling this entire process of impoverishment and economic formatting of the continent? Is such a process of impoverishment and formatting of Europe a "new order" associated to the full control of people, as wished by Obama (to avoid terrorism?)? John Perkins, who worked at the World Bank and the NSA, can help us to understand what happens: "This empire, unlike any other in the history of the world, has been built primarily through economic manipulation, through cheating, through fraud, through seducing people into our way of life, through the economic hit men. I was very much a part of that. (…) I worked very, very closely with the World Bank. The World Bank provides most of the money that's used by economic hit men, it and the IMF".

Franklin and Pessoa

The thoughts of two characters emerge as a kind of response to all that. The first one is very known of the American population, however strangely overlooked by contemporary Americans. He is Benjamin Franklin: "They who can give up essential liberty to obtain a little temporary safety deserve neither liberty nor safety." The second is a poet, Portuguese, better known in Europe, but less known than he should be. He is Fernando Pessoa: "If after I die, people want to write my biography, there is nothing simpler. They only need two dates: the date of my birth and the date of my death. Between one and another, every day is mine."

Errors

Now, we know that again – after we have received the same news few months ago - the IMF confesses a new mistake. It was wrong again especially in relation to Greece and Portugal. The error of the IMF caused the misery of millions of people, the fragmentation of families and the suicide of hundreds if not thousands of people. Who is responsible for that? On the other hand, the European Central Bank states that it did not made any mistake while participating in the same acts with IMF. How an international entity can say that it was wrong and the other one contradict it, saying that it was no error, on the same fact? Is someone lying? Is it a gamble? The European Union - also participant in the same acts - just is in silence. But, how the European Union could fail to start a criminal investigation into these confessed errors?

Mistakes

If a politician makes mistakes, he or she will suppos-edly pay for the error losing votes, or - as it should happen more often - going to prison. If a doctor errs, there will be a commission to judge him or her. There are even cases of judges who pay for their mistakes, although, unfortunately, it is very rare. If an ordinary citizen errs, he or she will face to serious problems. How can an entity with such responsibility and pow-er make so rude mistakes? What happened to the IMF as consequence of its confessed errors? Nothing. Because they sell just an "opinion". However, if the countries fail to follow it, it will the bankruptcy. Isn't that what we call blackmail?

Mistakes?

But, are you sure that really is about mistakes? The economist John Perkins thinks not. Much of Argen-tines and Brazilians, who have passed through the hands of the IMF, agree with Perkins. Where the IMF acted it often left a trail of misery and indignation. Worse, IMF's work, often nefarious, is paid at weight in gold by the people who will suffer from its mis-takes. And we should not forget that both Greece and Portugal are dependent on other countries in terms of food and energy. If they not agree with the IMF, the ECB and the EU, they will simply stop receiving money borrowed and will not have food to eat, as well as no heating in the winter - many don't know, but the north of Portugal, for example, is covered by snow during periods in winter. That is, these countries are kidnapped. Their economic development have been intensively monitored by the EU for decades. Surprisingly, the same EU says not knowing what happened during that period! Has EU no responsibility for its works over decades?

Embezzlement

The European Central Bank said it was not wrong. The European Union is quiet. So let's see: both the situation of Greece and that of Portugal have some similarities. In both countries the size of the State is excessive, government debt is huge, both countries are heavily dependent on foreign countries, their governments are often accused of corruption by the press, the judiciary doesn't work - mainly because of the huge periods of time required to arise a sentence, and much of the countries are - directly or indirectly - depend on the respective States. There are a lot of accusations made by the press showing that both countries were victims - as denounced by the Spanish popular movements - of gigantic crimes of embezzlement by politicians.

Juridical order

How to change this situation? Initially, it will be replacing the juridical order. Ie, analyzing the contracts made by the governments in the last twenty years, many of them certainly odious, and therefore with no legal value, and canceling those that are not correct. But such a measure is never adopted - probably because who is involved in those contracts are the financial system and the same authorities, political or otherwise, that are now elected as saviors of that countries!

Economic structure

How to change such a disastrous framework in countries like Greece and Portugal? The answer will be: changing the economic structure of these countries. Firstly, it is not something that can be done in four or five years without killing the country. Secondly, all countries in the European Union today perfectly knew how the so-called "southern countries" were and behaved when they "joined the club". No one is innocent in this story. Much of the debt was made in partnership and on behalf of so-called "correct countries" like Germany.

Bureaucracy

But, even so - if we could forget that everything seems to be mounted on a terrible and mafioso network of economic interests, where people are the victims - ... but, how to change that situation? Firstly, eliminating to the maximum bureaucracy. This will require the implementation of a new subsidy policy, because bureaucracy is just an instrument for distributing money to unskilled labor. However, the distribution of subsidies should be a responsible mechanism with goals, attending the population - and not like bureaucracy, which is totally irresponsible as economic instrument. Interestingly, no one until now seems to have questioned the responsibility of bureaucracy as an economic instrument.

Taxes

Another step is the elimination of taxes to boost economy and increase tax revenue. The reduction of the State will come next. You cannot suddenly reduce a big State without destroying the population. The decline of the State cannot be a process of annihilation of the population. If so, it will be innocuous because it will eliminate the nation. Those institutions, like the several States around the world, should work for the people, and never against them. Everyone knows that it should be like that, even the IMF, the ECB or the EU.

Frog in water

What the IMF and the ECB did? They dramatically increased taxes in those countries, imposing a brutal downsizing liquidity and decreasing tax revenues. They did not question politicians, many of them corrupt and criminals according to the journalism media. They increased even more bureaucracy, creating more barriers to private initiative and inhibiting foreign investment. All this meant that countries had to ask even more borrowed money, did not create a domestic consumption market and started being cheap exporters. They turned negative interest rates, eliminating savings and impoverished populations. They increased facilitation to irresponsible credit. In this way, the debt - public and private - exploded, the countries entered in misery, stopped producing and creating wealth. The most curious is that the protests are relatively few. As if everyone was sound asleep and everything was gradually impoverishing like the water warms up killing a frog without him being aware of what is happening.

Respect and time

Respect as an element emerged from time, is one of the fundamental conditions in economy. Such element, so often overlooked, determines the design of the market. Respect, as we conceptualize it, acquires body with the Enlightenment in the 18th century as a result of the intensive and specialized use of vision through Gutenberg's press. Book requires time and attention, while real-time eliminates both of them.

Vulgarization

When I was young there was a clothes store in the corner of Park Ave and 54th Street, in New York City, called Syms. Its slogan was "An Educated Customer is our Best Customer". Even my parents where used to go there. The store closed its doors few years ago. Unlike what happened before in European and major U.S. cities, like New York, the beginning of the 21st century is marked by the absolute vulgarization of the urban centers. So, to be at the Fifth Avenue became like to be in some neighborhood of Caracas, in downtown Sao Paulo or even in Paraguay. The big difference was eliminated because, in general and everywhere, people no longer have respect.

Directors

The criterium for selecting directors and curators in major universities, museums and cultural institutions both in America and in Europe, is now - exclusively - money. Thus, people might have good links with the financial world in order to drive a museum like the Metropolitan in New York City, a university like Harvard, Georgetown and so on. Sometimes these directors and curators are so uneducated that they are not even able to properly hold a fork. Lack of respect.

Frontiers

Go through some national frontiers, like the Italian ones, can be a disastrous experience, even to the best-intentioned tourist. Border guards, sometimes taken out of misery, are commissioned by the illegal money they find. It is the complete failure of the police system. So, everybody immediately became guilty until proven otherwise. Those policemen, often remarkably ignorant, can address to the traveler the most varied types of humiliation, embarrassing questions, and even compromise the next trip without any plausible justification, and without any right or instance for effective claim by the tourist. A complete collapse of the rule of law. And no one protests. All this means lack of respect.

Crimes

No government is mandated for the crime. And no people can be held responsible for crimes committed in their name but without their full consent. The worst: associated to the financial system, various governments have been clearly linked to crimes, blaming their own peoples, enriching their politicians, and leading national salvation plans - performed by those same politicians and the same financial systems - further increasing the debts of their countries, and affecting several generations. All this can possibly be articulated with an economic war. Both facts are not contradictory. Protests are relatively few, especially if we take into account the extension of the committed crimes. Why? Because of a widespread lack of respect.

Food

Around the year 2000 the price of a barrel of oil suddenly rose about four times and remained establishing a new level. And no one wondered if such event was, in fact, the formation of a large international cartel. Prices of pharmaceuticals are absolutely abusive - even taking into account the argumentation that they feed scientific research. There is a clear promiscuity between doctors and pharmaceutical companies - constantly condemned by the international press. The famous journalism television program 60 Minutes reported the precarious situation, to say the least, of the FDA Food and Drug Administration of the United States, which was one of the most respected institutions in the world. Very expensive restaurants in Paris - before very respected - started selling industrialized food outrageously approaching fast-food. No one reacts. Why? Lack of respect.

Education and fortunes

In virtually all over the world there are constant denounces regarding the impoverishment of education standards. Many museums around the world do not have equipment or even funding for artists - but their directors earn fortunes. Why? Lack of respect.

Middle Ages

Thus, the elimination of time, leading to the lack of respect, redraws the market, producing a world of slaves, or quasi slaves, as well as ignorant and moneyed elites, very similar to what happened during the Middle Ages.

Economy of time

Karl Marx argued that "comprehensive social as well as individual development, consumption, and activity depend on the saving of time. All economy is ultimately an economy of time. Economy of time, like the planned distribution of work time among various branches of production, is still the first economic law based on collective production." Then, he and Engels started the concept called Economy of Time.

Lost of time

We've always heard that time is money. Interestingly, people in general, following Marx's thoughts, conclude the opposite – in exclusive terms: that time is inversely proportional to wealth, so you should never "waste time". But "time is money" literally means "the more time, more money." Thus, although Marx is right, such doesn't have an exclusive nature. Absolute reduction of time nullifies economy. Zero time also is zero economy.

Impact

Often we do not realize the impact of time on economy. Books, especially classic literature, require a good amount of time. Hours are devoted to a good book. In the late nineteenth century, gradually, fashion started focusing on magazines, like almanacs, requiring less time. The first half of the twentieth century was dominated by newspapers with even less time. Hence, it moved to radio and television, with almost instantaneous time. Finally, we arrived to computers and to real time.

Short time

Before, we were used to write letters - often with two, three or more pages. Then, people first made drafts and only after all corrections made the letters were really "written." The letters became electronic mail. Email messages require much less time. Gradually, people began reducing the signs in emails in order to turn them into an almost exercise of stenography. But it was not enough. Soon social networks appeared and people reduced even more the time with shorter messages. Then we had Tweeter, where messages with up to 14 syllables. And memory was erased.

Fast

Electricity and with it the telephone were the major drivers of this process. In this way, food became fast-food in big cities. Classical music, which before lasted several minutes, turned into pop, with about three minutes in average. Television series, which lasted twenty minutes for decades, were reduced to four minutes per chapter. It appeared the so-called "fast theater", with only five minutes. Books with many pages began to be abandoned.

Acceleration

In terms of economics, the old long-term pattern of savings, typical in the social role of banks, in the value of work and education, was replaced by the short time of accelerated metabolism: negative interest rates, elimination of savings, end of the value of work, end of attention and end of education. In a world without time, the person disappears. Everything becomes blind and dumb emergence of the process of acceleration, without memory.

Respect

The word "respect" etymologically means "double attention", to "look carefully". A world without time is a world without capital, without money, where - in apparent contradiction - everything becomes aspiration to money. No more human values, because there is no time, no attention and no memory. Without time surplus labour disappears and everything becomes aspiration to it, in the smallest behaviors: everybody starts aspiring to "easy money".

IQ

Studies by Dr. Jan te Nijenhuis, professor of work and organizational psychology at the University of Amsterdam, suggest human intelligence is on the decline. His studies indicate that Westerners have lost 14 I.Q. points on average since the 19th century. And the decline of intelligence is related to time. In late 19th Century, visual reaction times averaged around 194 milliseconds. In 2004 that time had grown to 275 milliseconds. We can conclude that less time of reflection retarded visual time reaction.

Three parts

Here we find an interesting relationship between time, economy and intelligence. Eliminating the first, you will inevitably erase the other two - because economy is not reduction of means, but yes implicitness of terms.

Less time

According to a survey published in April 2006 by consumer analysts at the Henley Centre of the University of Reading, in the United Kingdom, people value time more than they do money. Around 41% of respondents mentioned time as their most valuable resource, while only 18% believed that money was most important. Less time, more valued it is.

Low cost

If you try claiming against low cost airlines, against social networks like FaceBook, or often even against services from the State, you will certainly find a huge barrier. Try to make a phone call to a telecommunications company - to complain about a service, for example – and, inevitably, you will find an electronic barrier made of endless recorded questions, a maze that many times ends in nothing. This is one of the visible faces of a fabulous and fast planetary transformation: the domain of big corporations.

An automatic phenomenon

When such domain happens, there is no longer individual right and everything is overrun by bureaucracy. You may wonder what is the reason. The answer is simple: the relative cost of a set of well-paid lawyers for a large company is negligible, but for an individual the cost of a few hours of an attorney is sometimes prohibitive. Thus, dominating the economic fabric, large companies and corporations automatically establish the "noise" that benefit them. There is no intention in this process. It is an automatic phenomenon.

Rights

Everything is a matter of scale. Also through an automatic process, large companies corrupted the already corrupt political world. On the other hand, the process of political selection favored the less capable but more eager. Thus, the State became a part of the business process. So the person was transformed into taxpayer and consumer. The individual no longer has any value, and almost no rights in his small scale. Just imagine entering with a legal action against a big corporation.

The time of big corporations

But this is not new. It is, in fact, an old story. This also happened with the feuds in the Middle Ages. Then, there was no possibility of individual claim or even of his participation. There were revolts. The same thing happened with the monarchies. And we had revolutions. Then the same phenomenon happened with totalitarian regimes. And they ended in misery. Now it seems that is the time of big corporations.

Pope

Normally, who makes a similar warning is adept at any Marxist dogma. But, in general, such people criticize in order to establish another dictatorship. I do not have any kind of political alignment. I'm free. And the economic dictatorship established by large corporations is enormous - with a so fast progression that even Pope Francisco manifested his worries about it.

The opposite

A few days ago the value of gold knew another record devaluation. Now, another crash happened. The actor and television host, Jon Stewart - whom I greatly admire - insinuated in his daily program that the fall of gold would have been a good punishment for speculators and ridiculed those who have questioned about its reason. Jon Stewart is not an economist and the reasons of the gold fall are really obscure. In those same days, newspapers around the world reported that China was buying massive amounts of gold. So? How could the value drop? A couple of days before the fall of gold Goldman Sachs advised its customers to quickly sell their assets in gold, accordingly to the Bloomberg article published on April 15. There are many shadows and we do not know if an involvement of Goldman Sachs and China really happened, or even if the bank was responsible, even partially, by the falling value of gold. What we know is that Goldman Sachs is a giant financial institution, and it is extremely aggressive. It is its nature - if not, it would not be big. Beyond speculation - not as intended Jon Stewart, but about large corporations speculating - there is no rational explanation for the fall of gold: interest rates are negative, Europe and the United States are on the verge of bankruptcy, taxes are more and more higher, the estimated size of annual gold market is of about five trillion dollars, banks are increasingly unsafe, and there is a growing demand for gold by various countries. Everything points to exactly the opposite.

Other theses

There are however two other theories that have been launched in various newspapers and media worldwide. The first, most famous, argues that it is about the explosion of a gold bubble. But if it was true, gold would not oscilate so much. When there is a bubble, the object of its explosion just falls, deeply depreciates. But what we have is a process of valuing and devaluing, creating waves. When we have those waves, we are inside a traditional context of speculation. The other theory is conspiratorial and argues that the United States is undermining the value of gold in way to avoid the return of a gold standard. But now we are dealing with a gold market of about five trillion dollars. Knowing the disorganization and incompetence of governments in general, it seems more likely to be about an intensely speculative operation on certificates with the aim of benefiting gangs of investors - however they deserved another name.

Kennedy

People are questioning among themselves, but the individual has been increasingly with less rights. This reminds me of John Fitzgerald Kennedy when he said: "Those who make peaceful revolution impossible will make violent revolution inevitable." It's just a lesson of history.

Health

Health is one of the essential elements of economy. Not only it is essential in itself - because a population without health doesn't produce and doesn't participate in the market – but also because it turned out to create its own market, contrarily to its very first nature. Someone can imagine a military or a religious person as a millionaire? Why not? Because the logic of those activities doesn't operate through averages. On the other hand, capitalism operates large averages. If an army is in "the middle" it is a loser army, it will fail. Also religion cannot be "in the middle", if not it will be nothing. The same applies to education, to culture and to health.

Games

Amid a voracious ignorance, the political world goes ahead blind, not understanding that the world cannot be imperiously oriented by a single logic. The logic of capitalism, in its natural principle of zero-sum game, doesn't work in army, religion, education, culture and health. In these universes, the essential principle is that of non-zero-sum game.

Cartels

In Switzerland, health care costs are exorbitant. There, medical treatment can lead a person into bankruptcy. The same happens in the United States. In both countries, a person without health insurance is literally in risk of life. In Switzerland, health insurance is tremendously expensive and compulsory. Many things in Switzerland eventually became cartelized, kidnapping people. The same is happening in the United States. The plans for a widespread public health in the United States are very similar to what happens in Switzerland which generated a large cartel of few insurance companies.

Medical inflation!

Some years ago, a new trend has emerged: the so-called defensive medicine. It proposes to protect doctors from possible accusations of malpractice and subsequent lawsuits by their customers. In fact, it spawned a voracious industry of lab tests, often unnecessary. Many doctors came to be commissioned by medical laboratories. Values have risen astronomically. An annual check-up now can cost several times the minimum wage. The insurance companies pay for them. But who pays the insurance companies are us! And the value of an insurance policy is growing at a fantastic progression – to the point, ironically, that doctors and pharmacists have established a new economic index: a "medical inflation", contradicting the official inflation data.

Prefrontal

Why is all that happening? First, the knowledge, even intuitive, that different sectors work accordingly to different logics, depends on the prefrontal brain area. Do you remember what all of us always have said about the importance of education for the future? We never said that in reference to a religion or to some specific cuisine. We meant education as literacy. With new technologies, the volume of functional illiterates is increasing. The phonetic alphabet and paper, as has been exhaustingly demonstrated by philosophers and scientists, enhances the activity of the prefrontal brain area. Thus, translating: the world has been gradually invaded, everywhere, by ignorant people. These people can even dominate certain aspects of knowledge, but lack what we call "civilization." The defunctionalization of the prefrontal brain sector also intensifies what we call greed, by reducing the awareness of the other - cheerfully leading everyone to the cliff.

Serious reforms?

The structural economic reforms in Europe have the assumption that all those who participated in its previous order were and continue to be in good faith. But according to countless scandals and endless denunciations in the press, is not what happens. According to such denounces, people who had not a penny - really poor people – became politicians and quickly millionaires through the use of public money. And these are the same people who are ahead of reforms now! Who can believe they are serious people? How to believe, even people in the streets, that it is about serious reforms?

Odious contracts?

First, economic reforms in several countries, including the United States, have only caused more structural problems and have increasingly compromised the future of their populations, benefiting small and powerful interests groups. Credible economic reforms, even in the United States, should first identify those who benefit from them, the crimes they eventually represent or represented, to put away (at least) the criminals (it would be better to put them in jail), and firmly condemn in concrete terms any act of active or passive corruption. In this way, we would be able to clearly distinguish between contracts with legal value and those that are considered odious and that are, therefore, by its nature, null. On the other hand, criminal convictions should involve politicians and other people, entrepreneurs or lobbyists, involved in any act of corruption.

New slavery

Now let's look at a simple arithmetic: the large financial corporations have been responsible for all significant loans to States. We also know that they are associated to the IMF, the ECB and the Federal Reserve, participating in rescue plans, the famous bailouts. Many of these loans were accompanied or anticipated by acts of corruption, as has been reported by the world press. But who was in power at the time of these loans - ie the criminals – are now responsible for their renegotiation! Interestingly, with the renegotiation, debts increased even more - and in benefit of exactly those same financial corporations. The dues increased to the point of becoming impossible to be fully paid. So, the production of these countries, for decades to come, will be automatically allocated to pay debts to the international financial institutions.

But how to not call that slavery? What Constitution allows a politician or group of politicians to enslave the people?

Capitalism

On the other hand, political parties - without exception - have become committed to major financial corporations. This happens even to the so-called "left parties", that happily go to televisions to cry out against capitalism. But the fundamental question is not to be against capitalism, but to be against crime!

Interest rate

The European Central Bank has just decreed a further drop in interest rate director. We all know that it just means a strategy to transfer money from people to States, eliminating savings. The official inflation rate in Europe in January 2013 was about 2% per year. Although this data is most certainly a fraud, it is still much higher than the ECB rate director. Anyone who has a savings account, or some money in the bank – in the United States, Europe or almost any other country now - will be impoverished. Japan has followed this strategy dictated by the IMF since the 1990s, and since then only met recession. In this process the respective States grew stronger, and people impoverished, eliminating the dynamics of economy. There is another important question: knowing that reducing the interest rate, after a certain limit, erodes economy, who benefits from this strategy? A question for a simple answer: those same large financial corporations claiming the debt.

Social role of banks

What is more interesting is that the brutal decline in interest rates - below the official inflation and well below the actual inflation – just destroyed the old social role of banks and turned them into purely speculative entities.

Reality

All this to say: almost anything that States and political economists in power have said never coincides with reality.

New York

The Administration of New York City presented a report, made by Mark Levitan, which shows that almost half of the inhabitants of Manhattan were in poverty in 2011. Apparently, the situation has only worsened since then.

France

Now, the French magazine Capital announced the results of a survey lfop, showing that about 70% of the French population believe the country will enter in a social upheaval. The number increases to 81% among those classified as "workers"!

Brazil

Brazil considers, officially, that the limit of extreme poverty in the country is around two dollars per day per family! Considering the number of people in a Brazilian family around four, to be in great poverty each one should receive twenty-five cents per day. No wonder there are no many poor people in Brazil... everybody jumped to middle-class.

Ministers

In her statement of assets, Marisol Touraine, Minister of Social Affairs and Health in the socialist presidency of François Hollande, declared that she had only the equivalent of less than three minimum wages in her five French bank accounts! Yamina Benguigui, Minister of Francophony (!), declared two bank accounts in zero, with no money. Laurent Fabius, secretary of state in this government and former French Prime Minister, recognized millionaire by the media - with millions of dollars in properties, owner of a wonderful collection of ancient art, declared he was in debit... his account was overdrawn. The same happened to Christiane Taubira, Minister of Justice (!): one of her bank accounts was declared negative.

Harvard

Basically, the theory of Carmen Reinhart and Kenneth Rogoff was that after the 90% debt related to the GDP, economic growth dramatically decreases and strangles the country. This theory has been used by the IMF and the ECB as essential reference to justify the drama that is happening in Europe. If that was true, Brazil would have never recovered from its crisis of the 1980s. And it only recovered when refused to follow the IMF orders. The most interesting is that Thomas Herndon, Michael Ash and Robert Pollin eventually proved that Reinhart and Rogoff were wrong. But how the two Harvard professors did not know they were wrong?! The error was obvious! How could they not know? Their letter of justification is not clear or justifiable.

GDP

What has been announced by governments as GDP is a fraud. Fundamentally, until the 1970s, GDP was calculated as the result of what the country produced less what it imported. After the 1980s, it became to be the result of what the country produces added to what the state consumes, subtracting what it imports. If a state spends on a non-sense advisory service, losing money... it will be considered as income! Thus, the thesis of Reihnart and Rogoff could never be correct simply because GDP is a fraud, and they should know it!

Inflation

Inflation stopped being calculated on an average of consumed products, and started being based on a restricted basket of essential products... that can be subsidized – it is a fraud.

Central Banks

The European Central Bank announced that it would reduce the interest rate again, to almost zero, similar to what the United States did. But, after a certain level, very low interest rate ceases to be beneficial to the country and starts eroding and eliminating the savings, affecting responsibility on loans, serving as a form of cheap financing way for states and large corporations - using citizen's money - and destroying economy. How economists do not know this? The vice president of the European Central Bank is a Portuguese, Vitor Constancio, who was previously president of the Bank of Portugal. Shortly before leaving the country, under his direction, the Bank of Portugal sold good part of its gold reserves... immediately before the big increase of gold value. The country has lost a lot of money. His departure was disturbed by fraud scandals or, at best, accusations of incompetency. Immediately after he was awarded the vice-presidency of the European Central Bank.

Exportation

Another myth is the exportation. Most governments announce that exportation is the salvation. But exportation, after a certain limit starts consuming the capital of the country. Like subsidies, exportation is an excellent protection against the turmoils of cyclical economic environment. Like what happens in mechanics of fluids.

Tyranny

Thomas Jefferson said, "Experience has shown, that even under the best forms of government those entrusted with power have, in time, and by slow operations, perverted it into tyranny."

Revolution

If there will be a planetary revolution, like the French expect, the people in the streets will destroy the rulers, and soon after, by a historical order, also the innocent people, as an apparent justifiable form of theft.

Paying the robbery

Wolfgang Schäuble, Germany's finance minister, said: "The participation of shareholders, holders of subordinated bonds and, after, depositors of unsecured deposits will become the norm when a financial institution will fall into a difficult situation."

No jail

The current situation is as follows: virtually all banks stopped paying interests, or the interests are negative - given the accounts maintenance costs; investments became so risky that do not compensate the little profit they offer; commodities are more and more subject to the volatility of global speculation promoted by powerful groups of interests. The states do not stop raising taxes and administrative costs through a growing bureaucracy. Real Estate as investment became another target of the States, subject to a constant increase in taxes. On the other hand, the monetary base growth appears to have no end. In this context, Schauble's disastrous declaration - which manifests serious doubts about his technical skills – is equivalent to a big warning: "Everybody, take all your money from the banks. Not only they are not paid, but also they may be used to cover disasters caused by the theft of their directors"- who, incidentally, apparently never end up in jail.

Chaos

If people heed the call of Wolfgang Schauble, the European financial system would simply shut down and plunge the continent into chaos.

Interest rates

The base interest rate of the European Central Bank is 0.75% per year, and that one of the Federal Reserve in the United States is 0.25% per year. Both the United States and Europe have devastated economies, with high unemployment, a growing corrosion of real wages and with their administrative systems virtually in bankruptcy. In this context, the president of the German central bank (Bundesbank), Jens Weidmann, has announced that interest rates will only be changed if the situation will get worse! And surely, he thinks to change down, probably to 0% per year!

Monetary Base

The Central Bank of Japan announced that it will promote the doubling of the monetary base over the next two years, following the same procedure taken by the United States and Europe.

Work and economy

What is the solution for this disastrous situation? First, one must distinguish between real and odious debt. Then establish a plan for economic growth to meet the debts. This economic growth can not be sustained on credit but yes on an increase in the real value of labor income. To do so, we must reduce taxes, thereby increasing revenue. Should also increase the base interest rate, increasing the fitting of new funds, giving function and responsibility to the credit. More than that - these measures support the spirit of work, without which there is no economy.

Music

Another day in Paris, a fabulous organ concert, performed by one of the leading organists in the world with a rare program with pieces by Bach, performing in one of the best organs in the world, at Ille de Saint Louis, had little more than twenty people in the audience - though it was free. In New York City, at the same time, a brilliant French quartet visiting the city, specialized on contemporary music, with two world premieres on the program, conducted in a small but prestigious theater in town, had less than thirty people in the audience.

Equilibrium Points

Although both of them were events of major importance, none of the most important newspapers, TV stations and magazines have published anything about them - neither before nor after. The excuse is that there are so many cultural activities in these cities that would not be possible to write about all. But this is not true. The fact is that journalists and editorial directors consider that this kind of event "has a small market", ie they do not represent a "big audience" and that therefore do not attract large number of readers. Or, in other words, they "do not represent a lot of money." When everything is based solely on money, economy ends - as brilliantly demonstrated by the economist John Nash, Nobel Prize in 1994, with his celebrated thesis Equilibrium Points in n-Person Games.

Brazil and Italy

In a place as far away as Brazil, the main newspaper of the country closed its most important sector of culture and has become specially focused on corrupt politicians, social quarrels and the unsurpassed superficiality of television reality shows. In Italy, people more cultured and aware cry seeing the cultural heritage of thousands of years without care, virtually abandoned. All in name of money - ignoring Nash's law.

Louvre

Last Wednesday, the world's largest museum, the Louvre in Paris, closed its doors due to a strike by the security guards of the museum. The reason was the increase of burglars and uncontrollable violence. David Malliard, responsible for the union of museums in Paris, said: "Guards and visitors are victims, every day, of pick-pockets and violence." Alexandra Kardianou, secretary of the CGT of Louvre, added: "It's getting worse: the thieves start in the subway... Thieves' networks have a quasi-military organization. " Few weeks before, the city of Paris was frightened by the large increase in a phenomenon that was previously restricted to countries like Brazil, the organized gang looting: dozens of thugs invading the subway, assaulting and injuring its users. The number of criminals is so great that the local security can do nothing.

Education and Economic Impact

All over the world, the levels of education are falling – particularly regarding primary education, of children. In 2012, the Wall Street Journal warned: the decline in education in the United States is beginning to represent a strong and negative economic impact. According to a research conducted at Harvard University by Claudia Goldin and Lawrence Katz, Americans born in 1955 received an average of more two years of schooling than their parents. But those born in 1980 studied only eight months more than the parents. And all indications are that this trend will become increasingly pronounced, tending to a reduction in standards of education relatively to the previous generations.

Education and Politicians

In Brazil, the trend is reversed - but it may be a false appearance. There, as it has happened in several European countries, repetition was eliminated in the early years of schooling. The reason is that in this way students will have a continuum of learning, with no stress. But in fact such strategy showed that the number of students with good academic success suddenly increased dramatically, not representing reality - but enriching panels of political propaganda. Gradually, the homework has also being eliminated - to encourage those who, for one reason or another, do not study. In Europe, the Treaty of Bologna, reduced the period of undergraduate college to only three years!

China

From the other side of the planet, China is heavily investing in the purchase of all planetary resources. The invasion of Tibet had no different reason: Tibet is the main source of water for China, supplying the country - with water from the melting of its glaciers – in more than 50% of its needs. China began its buying strategy of world natural resources in Africa, but quickly spread throughout the world.

Gandhi and Nash

Mahatma Gandhi once said, "In matters of conscience, the law of the Majority has no place." Such a thought might be an interesting principle of economy, in full conformity with the ideas of John Nash.

The Law and the individual

As is well known, not only by experts, one of the most sacred pillars of the rule of law is the principle of presumption of innocence. In history, only the most sordid totalitarian regimes despised it. It is - as it is also well known even by relatively uneducated people - about a principle established by societies with a strong literary and visual nature. This principle is inextricably linked to the concepts of the individual and of isonomy, according to which all are equal before the law. Therefore - according to these principles - who pay the taxes, which should never be high enough to become confiscation, should have full ownership and plain rights over his property, being free to do whatever he wants with it, because an individual can only exist in its fullness with the power to freely dispose of what belongs to him.

Two hundred years

Once taxes paid, the remaining is the person's legitimate property. This has been the understanding of the law over the past two centuries at least. This scenario is an essential one of a free society, when it has the rule of law as its structural element. Only the tyranny, whether theological or secular in nature, can repudiate this scenario, without, however, being able to deny its truth. However, even during the last two hundred years, such rule has not been always clear.

Latin America

I remember the 1960s and the 1970s, especially the terrible military dictatorships in South America, and more especially the regimes in Argentina and Brazil, when it was openly said that nothing, not even the money, belonged to the person. The citizen was, then, a figure in transition, only a faithful depositary of what ultimately belonged to the State. Even paying taxes, anyone could be suddenly stripped of all his possessions. This reality deeply horrified the open societies of the West. It was enough - in Europe or in the United States – to read what happened in Latin America to classify those countries dominated by tyranny as underdeveloped and very uncivilized. Now, at the beginning of the 21st century, the dark shadows of totalitarianism seem to gradually reemerge.

A threat to democracy

The first page of the French newspaper Le Monde today, April 5, 2013, brings a disconcerting editorial article that, therefore, speaks on behalf of the newspaper. Titled "The offshore system, this patented enemy of democracy," the text states that "tax havens are a threat to democracy. They undermine the rule of law on playing on the concealment"- a statement as false as deeply disturbing. The threat to democracy is the change in our mental structure or, in other words, the transformation of our values, what sets our reality. In neurological terms, what threatens democracy is a change in the mode of functionalization of the called prefrontal sector in our brains, which is responsible for the idea of "individual," among other fundamental concepts to democracy. The threat to democracy is not in the existence of free and independent countries with lower taxes! Everyone knows that there is no banking secrecy in Switzerland or in offshore countries for crimes - provided there is an order of a court, which is very reasonable. On the other hand, one could argue that the structures of offshore companies and Trusts operate in chain, hiding their true owners. But this is something that has continuously happening over thousands of years - just take a trip to the Amalfi Coast and see the caves used to hide assets during the Middle Ages. One solution would be to arrest all people, but obviously this is not admissible. The argumentation of Le Monde in its editorial is a remarkable declaration of incompetence of the police to identify and prosecute criminals. Not having the ability to do so, the State simply annuls one of the fundamental principles of the rule of law and equally preventively classifies all persons as criminals until proven otherwise.

Aristotle and Lord Acton

Wherever we find a State in the beginning of this century, it seems that inevitably we will always find corruption - and the States do not stop growing! This phenomenon gives reason to Aristotle when he said that "power corrupts" but gives even more reason to Lord Acton when he said: "absolute power corrupts absolutely." There are critics who, with apparent reason, criticize the fact that the exposition of such a situation would produce an obvious risk to democracy, because when people discredit the democratic regime, they would automatically embrace dictatorship (according to those critics). But here too the problem is another: the risk to democracy is not in the denunciation, in the direct fight against criminals, but yes in the impunity.

Denunciation

When a false reason is established as truth, crime is strengthened. If in place to make his crusade against a fake goal, like the offshore companies, the French newspaper perform a hard and direct combat against the corruption in the government of its own country, and if the local courts worked well, surely successive governments would drop and probably even the newspaper itself would close its doors ... and these possibilities say, by themselves, about the actual situation.

World scenarios

But this scandalous article of the French newspaper is not, unfortunately, an isolated case. Switzerland prepares to vote, in the second half of 2013, a set of laws that are retroactive! If this happens, jurisprudence will gradually destroy everything we know as citizens' rights, approaching the west to despotic societies dominated by a theological system. Nowadays, a Frenchman who wants to move to another country is not allowed to sell his own home without sharing with the State the sale proceeds – the confiscation is justified, as if it could be justified, with the excuse that the person in question would no longer pay taxes in the country. In the United States, an American who decides to give up his nationality and move to another country will have to pay a fine equivalent to the taxes that he would pay until his presumable death - everything is rigorously calculated by the State, taking into account the average life expectancy, education and the profession of the person and even his salary and incomes at the time of the decision. They are, very unfortunately, scenarios very similar to those experienced in the reality of totalitarian dictatorships in Latin America in the 1960s and 1970s.

Colonizers of Nations

When, in the 1970s and 1980s, there was the withdrawal, even partial, of England and France, and the total withdrawal of Portugal, some African countries became "colonized" by the United States and other ones by the Soviet Union. Then, the condition for a foreign person or corporation to create a business in those countries - especially those under Soviet protection - was to give, without any compensation, 51% of the companies to their respective states. This rule is still valid in many of those countries. But now, when we look at what happens in the so-called Western countries, we realize that the sum of taxes on a business far exceeded the 51%! Thus, taking the old rule applied in Africa, indeed the Western states were gradually nationalizing all companies, not by way of management and responsibility, but by way of participation in business through taxes. The States became gigantic sleeping partners, without investment, just beneficiaries of a system that greatly resembles the criminal organizations like the Mafia. That is, the States became colonizers of the Nations.

Patrolling

But this phenomenon was not restricted to companies – to have an apartment for rent in New York City has become, for example, one of the worst business in the world, so high are the taxes, fees and maintenance costs. The most curious thing is that those few who denounce this whole outrageous situation usually are immediately classified as right-wing dictators, becoming patrolled, monitored and censored. And there is not the slightest hint of indignation against all these facts.

Unconsciousness?

What Natalie Nougayrède - the editor of Le Monde - had an obligation to know, even to not be accused of propaganda in a environment that should excel for impartiality, is that the real threat to democracy is revealed by her own words - not through content, not because of the existence of free countries that charge less tax, but simply because a publisher of a major newspaper in the world apparently is not able to understand the real threats to democracy and broadcast a speech that only reinforces and supports those same threats, as if she is not aware of doing so!

Crusade and asphyxia

Then, after the angry shouts against actor Gerard Depardieu, we are surprised – unfortunately not too much - by the official scandals like those involving Jean-Jacques Augier or the French Minister Jérôme Cahuzac (incidentally, one of the strongest voices against Depardieu) who, after have lied, confessed to have an offshore account. But despite stoned in France, everyone knows (including Le Monde) that Depardieu received his money from work and paid the due taxes. Interestingly, the newspaper seems to be fairly condescending to anything that threatens the State and announces a fierce crusade - apparently in coordination with other newspapers - against offshore companies, however, without combating the asphyxiating condition that France has built with its super bureaucratic State and its declared fiscal terrorism. Did they forget what happened to the Soviet economy left in tatters by totalitarian measures to which France seems to get closer and closer?

The defense of freedom

Without the rule of law the only economy that can exist is that of the State, not of the citizens, as History showed us so many times. Here it is not about a defense of the offshore companies, of the Trusts, or of any mechanism for concealment of property. It is the firm defense of the rule of law. If there were not such a defense, we would quietly and willingly accept the reducing of the fundamental rights and freedoms in response to terrorist attacks, for example. And such is simply inadmissible, unacceptable. Here it is about, rather, the defense of the principles of civil liberty hardly erected over thousands of years.

Mistakes?

Virtually every day, we witness bizarre and confusing statements from politicians - often simply ignorant people in power - and even from economists, many times famous members of important institutions. But we should always seek coherence in life: When a famous cook makes mistakes of beginners, or worse, we suspect: he's sick, is a charlatan or did it intentionally and is a criminal. How might so many economists today be sick at the same time?

Cyprus

We witnessed the infamous confiscation conducted by the "plan of salvation" in Cyprus in March 2013. Immediately, Jeroen Dijsselbloem - Dutch Minister of Finance and President of the Eurogroup - said in an interview that the confiscation in Cyprus would be a "template" for future EU Bailouts. Dijsselbloem's statement - which sparked an even greater crisis in

Europe - is so alarming that impresses by being an index havoc in Europe or just a big lie. In the first case, to be true, Dijsselbloem would be a criminal accomplice in an attack on the European economy. If not true, he would be incompetent or ill. In the second case, if it is about a big lie, Dijsselbloem would be a criminal working against the economic interests of Europe, or an incompetent who does not know what he says. Quickly, he denied what he had said. But serious doubts about what he is remain in the air – about which only history will be able to reveal.

Incompetence and crime

But what impresses indeed, is how a person who commits a so huge mistake, a so flagrant incompetence - or a so obvious crime - becomes minister of a country like the Netherlands and President of the Eurogroup!

Ponzi-schemes, taxes and credit

Firstly, it is important to understand what has happened in the world in recent decades. Between 1960 and 2008, in less than 50 years, the global wealth was multiplied 45 times! But gradually after the 1970s - through taxes from different natures and monetary policies - the real value of incomes has been shrinking - reducing the purchasing power of people. During this period, to keep the level of consumption, governments were inducing a facilitation of credit by banks, and an apparent increase of liquidity through financial institutions by removing control over "Ponzi-schemes". Thus, interest rates dramatically fell and counterparts for loans were literally being eliminated. The result is that people joined en masse to easy credit as to offset the decrease in real income. Whose responsibility is it? What is the purpose of an action like this? Obviously, it is not to save the country.

Continuous credit

A society strongly based on credit can be quickly enslaved. People in permanent debt can be maneuvered easily and flexibly. In a society of continuous credit, everyone is automatically guilty and is permanently subject to the power of the lender.

Lender and borrower

But, in many countries, if someone lends money at high interest rates and is stolen, he has no right to claim in court - because excessively high interest rates are indicators that something is wrong. So, the lender is co-responsible with the borrower.

Brazil

When Brazil experienced very similar situation with its banking system in the late 1980s, the Central Bank assumed its responsibilities and - through its monetary mechanisms - rebalanced the situation in time to save the country, not using taxes or confiscation to solve problems that monetary and economic policies had generated.

IMF

Why there is no responsible for the successive economic crimes? We all know the disaster that caused IMF in Argentina and Brazil (before the withdraw of the country, in Cardoso's government), in addition to several other countries. Now, again, the IMF – together with the EU and the ECB - is responsible for the management of European economic disaster. The measures are so clumsy that we are forced to ask ourselves if the technicians and officials of the IMF would all be sick, or whether they are criminals.

Perkins

Among many denounces, perhaps the most striking against the IMF comes from a former collaborator: John Perkins. His book Confessions of An Economic Hit Man is not only a bestseller, but also an overwhelming denounce. He explains what seems to be unexplainable. The question is: why no group of lawyers, in any country, never met to bring a lawsuit against the IMF in the Court of Human Rights? With so much evidence and so many denounces, why no one stands up against this institution? Why do we see politicians of all trends aligned with the IMF or, at best, in grim silence?

War

Thus, we see the rapid destruction of a continent. Across the world, China seems to encourage its satellite country - North Korea – to exercise the military muscles creating tension with the United States and consequently with Europe. The other satellite countries of China, Iran and Syria, are under pressure. In fact, it is about a clear destruction of European and American consumer markets, which fed China. It is a macabre hypothesis that revives the dangerous links between the Pentagon and the IMF, as warns John Perkins in his books.

Jean-Jacques Rousseau

Two statements by Jean-Jacques Rousseau marked my life. The first one, present in his classic master-piece The Social Contract is: "....in respect of riches, no citizen shall ever be wealthy enough to buy another, and none poor enough to be forced to sell himself." Rousseau wrote that in 1762, more than two hundred and fifty years ago. I question myself why the politi-cians and economists today still have not been able to realize the consequences of such a thought. The same could be said: if two people are starving in the desert, there is no place for charge of murder if one of them kills the other in order to survive.

Two Sides

Today, we find ourselves – in many countries around the world – as societies divided between the general population on one side, and politicians and big cor-porations in the other. This is the general picture.

And it represents a serious fracture of the Social Contract. Politicians and big corporations work primarily for themselves and create a process of brutal impoverishment of the middle class. On one side, the State, dominated by large corporations, allied to politicians, holds the legislative, judicial and executive powers - controlling, often, even the press, the fourth estate. On the other side, society is forced to pay for debts they did not contract.

Dictatorship

In this anti-political scenario, which spreads like fire in dry straw, critics – mostly of them politicians - warn about the risk of the emergence of a new scenario of spread of dictatorships. But isn't such a condition of break of the Social Contract a form of dictatorship?

Respect for Rights and Principles

No democracy, direct or representative, can survive if it does not respect a priori the human rights, the rule of Law and the state of Law. Even Switzerland is, at the beginning of the 21st century, in risk of losing its already classic status as respectable democracy, because of the gradual establishment of laws that offend those rights and principles.

Human Rights

The first four articles of the Universal Declaration of Human Rights say: "All human beings are born free and equal in dignity and rights.They are endowed with reason and conscience and should act towards one another in a spirit of brotherhood; Everyone is entitled to all the rights and freedoms set forth in this Declaration, without distinction of any kind, such as race, color, sex, language, religion, political or other opinion, national or social origin, property, birth or other status; Furthermore, no distinction shall be made on the basis of the political, jurisdictional or international status of the country or territory to which a person belongs, whether it be independent, trust, non-self-governing or under any other limitation of sovereignty; Everyone has the right to life, liberty and security of person; No one shall be held in slavery or servitude; slavery and the slave trade shall be prohibited in all their forms." The full text of the Universal Declaration of Human Rights can be read at http://www.un.org/en/documents/udhr/

State of Law

The State of Law is born from the Rechtsstaat, a doctrine in continental European legal thinking, originally borrowed from German jurisprudence, which can be simply translated as "state of Law." Some of its main principles are: "Civil society is equal partner to the State; Separation of the executive, legislative and judiciary powers; The judiciary and the executive powers are bound by law (no acting against the law), and the legislature is bound by constitutional principles; Both the legislature and democracy itself is bound by elementary constitutional rights and principles; Transparency of State acts and the requirement of providing a reasoning for all State acts; Review of State decisions and State acts by independent organs, including an appeal process; Hierarchy of laws, requirement of clarity and definiteness; Reliability of State actions, protection of past dispositions made in good faith against later State actions, prohibition of retroactivity; Principle of the proportionality of State's action."

Doom?

But, a little everywhere we see States breaking these Rights and principles, many times with the argumentation that they are saving the Nation. However, every time those Rights and principles are disregarded, we can be sure that doom is closer. What reminds me the other thought of Rousseau: "Every man has the right to risk his own life in order to preserve it. Has it ever been said that a man who throws himself out the window to escape from a fire is guilty of suicide?" - a thought that our politicians and economists should have always in mind.

Tax havens

So many times we see furious attacks and threats against countries known as "tax havens". The attacks are of two kinds: against people who have money there and directly against those countries. Attacks against people are unacceptable from a legal standpoint: because they affect the presumption of innocence, fundamental pillar of the rule of Law. And attacks against countries classified as "tax havens" are unacceptable because they attack another fundamental principle: that of the sovereignty of free nations.

Two attacks

In relation to the person, we should never confuse criminal and ordinary citizen. It is perfectly desirable that a criminal hiding money in a "tax haven" should be immediately persecuted. But virtually all "tax havens" have legal instruments to deliver criminals – of course if the proof of guilty is provided by a court.

How could a person be sentenced without judgement? The fact is that there is a total failure in police services all over the world and, then, serving as the easiest way, everyone started being automatically taken as potential criminal by authorities, eliminating the principle of the presumption of innocence. If a person made money and paid all taxes, the result is his property, and he has all freedom to move and use it as he wishes. But this is not the authorities' understanding because apparently they are not targeting the criminal, but yes the taxpayer. It is the struggle of the insatiable monster to absorb everything around, threatening even the rule of Law.

Robin Hood

Subjacent to this attack against people there are the miserable, hateful and demagogic "Robin Hood Fiscal Policies," which is the same to say: "taking from the rich to give to the poor." They are miserable, hateful and demagogic because they hurt another fundamental principle of the rule of Law according to which all are equal before the Law: isonomy. The fight against social asymmetry can never trample the principles of the sovereign rule of law.

Sovereignty

If we talk about the second type of attack, it is even more obscene. The UN Charter clearly states that all peoples have the right to self-determination. This principle is included the right to establish laws of any kind. Economists generally forget an essential element of economy: the scale. If small countries without skilled labor, no infrastructure and no raw materials in important quantities and qualities, establish the same fiscal framework of the so-called developed countries, they would immediately enter into bankruptcy. It is not to say about countries that protect criminals. But... everyone remembers very well the apparently promiscuous relationship between leaders of the called "advanced countries" and famous criminals like Muammar Gaddafi, for example.

Scale

The key issue, in both cases, is the scale. Just as a the tax structure of a "developed country" would be disastrous to a small one, "developed countries" structured in network no longer support the present tax principles. The already classical formulae "income tax," "taxes on consumption" etc.. simply ceased to function and be fair. They no long work because the so-called "rich" can easily move, and because consumption has limits determined by the scale of the person; and they are no longer fair because they establish a difference between people face to Law. Mechanic structure provided a person-to-person scale, which is now totally obsolete in our electronic world.

Capital Flow Tax

The only tax system that can operate on a global scale is that focusing on circulation of capital or, as I prefer call, on capital flow. It is fair, proportional and immediate, without bureaucracies, or persecutions. But the problem of this kind of tax is that it works in cascade, what is not allowed in many countries - because even their laws are outdated. This new type of taxation, even when applied in a very small percentage, quickly and very effectively replace all other ones, fighting social asymmetry without the need to appeal to obscene and demagogic persecution.

Hypocrisy and disintegration

In parallel to the hypocrisy of our politicians and so many economists, there is an increasing process of rupture and disintegration of our most valuable capital: the state of Law.

Globalization

The so-called globalization is a process of deep human interaction and cultural integration, all over the world. It is an important economic element. But even so there is a dark side. Intensifying the importation of what is cheaper - ie promoting the transfer of capital - an increasing devaluation of local workforce is generated. To some economists such phenomenon actually is a potential positive qualification process in medium and long term - because, due to competition, it would oblige local workforce to improve its productivity. But that can only happen if the countries where the products are imported from have similar conditions to those of the importing one, and especially if those exporting countries are not based on slave labor. If the reality of the exporting country is the slave labor, declared or not, the trend will inevitably be the transformation of the importing country's citizens also into slaves. Regardless, globalization also generates, by its nature, an increase of impoverishment, because with the importation of cheaper products there is an increased profit in the importing country that is not reinstated in the real economy of origin.

Capital and real economy

Capital has value only when it is integrated into the real economy. The absence of reinstatement in the real economy means greater concentration of income and greater social asymmetry. So when there is a re-location of production, there also is a relocation of capital, because the generated profit becomes concentrated and dislocated, increasing social asymmetry.

China

When China's integration into the WTO in 2001, many American and European companies have relocated their production there, just intensifying this phenomenon. That year I argued that the integration of China into the WTO, in the way it was established, would lead, quickly, to a deep crisis of liquidity in the Western world. The reasoning is very simple: when capital is took out from its environment, it is simply subtracted, canceled - this happens even if it has apparently grown. When profit is enormous but not reinstated, somehow, in real economy, it just disappears. Because capital is a relational function, not an absolute factor. When there is a relocation of industrial production to a place where labor market is much cheaper, despite the increase of profit, capital is no longer reinstated in its consumer society... and disappears. Thus, that importing society becomes increasingly poor. On the other hand, it is publicly known that the working conditions, social security and wage levels in China are so low, so bad, that the country is popularly - almost worldwide - considered immersed into a situation of real slavery. Because of this, the accelerated impoverishment of West became even more dramatic.

Concentration

Economist Robert Reich, former secretary of labor in Bill Clinton's administration, clearly shows, in his book Aftershock, a factor that caused not only the Depression of 1929 but also the Great Recession officially established in 2008: the immense concentration of wealth and consequent social asymmetry. In 1980, the richest 1% of Americans owned 9% of national income, in just about 25 years, that same 1% now owns almost 25% of the country's wealth: same index of 1928! Reich stated five principles for a healthy economy: that consumers can consume but also can save; companies have good conditions for investment; governments have a good balance between fiscal restraint (low taxes) and public needs; that economy can be distributed with balance over the entire society; and sustainability in environmental terms. None of this happens in virtually every country in the world at the beginning of the third millennium! This means that we are surely going fast to the abyss - contrarily to what government officials of several countries have said.

Communication technologies

There are other indicators that reinforce such a negative outlook. New communication technologies also have two faces. One of them presents us with a fabulous potential of social and cultural integration. On the other hand, new technologies of communication and informational treatment made possible the emergence of a world that is truly worthy of George Orwell: widespread surveillance, control and bureaucracy. These three elements reveal the complete failure of the police, for example, transferring to the citizen the burden of proof, reversing one of the fundamental principles of the rule of law: the presumption of innocence.

Noise in economy

Such reversal, establishing a large contingent of bureaucratic rules of control, implies the emergence of a heavy "noise" at the economic level. It is important to imagine the capital as something that obeys to a typical process of fluid mechanics, including turbulence. Like a liquid, capital automatically demands paths with fewer obstacles, with less "noise". The existence of barriers to economic flow generates turbulence and substantially reduces its dynamics.

Bureaucracy

Moreover, bureaucracy, in all its forms, represents a huge increase of costs. Just imagine this: when we have to fill out a form and are forced to be present in a public department, waiting for several minutes – or hours – to be attended, it is our man-hour cost that is at stake. In fact, it is about the cost of the bureaucratic system, with its staff and infrastructure, plus our own cost. Many of us have skills that project a high man-hour cost (even when we are doing something apparently free). However, revealing a gigantic and gross error, often the cost of each one of us in bureaucratic terms is considered zero by the State.

Subsidies

On the other hand, the political world has assigned to subsidies a demagogic fame of immoral act, with the argumentation that the State can not have paternalistic approaches. But subsidies are an important economic instrument - they represent a kind of stability tool against large economic fluctuations. And they should be applied to those sectors of society which intrinsic logic is not that one of the market - like health, education or culture. When subsidies disappear, they are usually replaced by more bureaucracy, which is, par excellence, an instrument of wealthy distribution. But, it is not effective – because it doesn't work on that fields; and it is highly expensive, paralyzing large sectors of society.

Representative democracy

Not only, beyond the disastrous scenario that characterizes virtually all economies in the beginning of the twenty-first century, there is the end of the social functions of representative democracy, what means that politicians started gravitating towards groups of interests. Such gravitation – called lobby in the US – triggers increasing tax distortions, and consequently increasing social asymmetry. With the end of the social functions of representative democracy politicians started working for themselves and not for the community. In such an environment, not only fiscal distortions started benefiting the larger companies, harming the smaller ones, as the increasing taxes started affecting specific sectors - seriously injuring another principle of the rule of law according to which all are equal before Law.

Tax increase and revenue

Of course, after a certain moment, tax increasing implies a reduction of revenue, as it was brilliantly showed by Arthur Laffer (following the ideas of Ibn Khaldun, who lived in the fourteenth century, and Keynes). However, to the politicians who are exclusively oriented to themselves, what counts is not the past or the future, but only the present - which can easily be translated by "anything goes." Thus the political universe, present in any power (executive, legislative or judiciary), became oriented to the ego-istic and immediate aims determined by its agents. With all this, big companies, conglomerates, and wealthy individuals simply stopped paying taxes, and the taxes applied to the middle class dramati-cally increased. The poorest sectors of the population also stopped paying taxes due to the growth of social asymmetries.

Consumption and concentration

There is another important factor to be considered: the consumption level of an individual is naturally limited. Thus, beyond a certain limit, tributary con-tribution becomes inevitably smaller. We only have two feet, two legs and the day has only 24 hours. Even so, the solution to this phenomenon would never be a tributary policy oriented to overwhelming levels of taxation to the richest – because it destroys the principle of isonomy; because you cannot clearly define the boundary line between the very rich and who is not so rich; and also because it creates a slow-ing factor in the economic system, working as a bar-rier - and, as we have seen, barriers are avoided by economic flows.

Migration

Another indicator of the disastrous economic real-ity is manifested in the migratory reality of many countries: the called non-integrated immigration. It is known that globalization intensifies migration. Before the telecommunication and information technologies, people who emigrated automatically switched off his previous environment. This disconnection induced a rapid integration into the new environment. But today, people do not disconnect from their place of origin, which makes them predatory immigrants, because – in an apparent paradox – they lose their identity and, also, they send good part of their incomes to their countries of origin, not contributing to local development. Although not integrated, they have voting rights - which makes many politicians, working for themselves, start managing legislative and fiscal systems in order to benefit this sector of the population which, through the votes, keep them in power. But that predatory population is focused only on their individual and selfish interests, not on the interests of the community. That represents more social costs and more taxes to the middle class.

Tax weight

To have an idea about where we arrived, in many countries the tax weight - added all taxes, not few of them happening in cascade - reaches 80% of the wealth! In France, in the case of higher incomes, only direct tax reaches 75%! In many countries the concept of tax income were expanded to goods and properties. In all these cases it is no longer about taxes, but about confiscation. Thus, the increasing and rapid elimination of the middle class produced a social proletarianization, the super bureaucratization generated general Sovietization, and the fiscal reality became confiscation.

Relocation and blackmail

Big companies started to relocate their production at higher speed, failing to contribute to the cultural and social local developments. Contrarily to what is commonly defend by corrupted politicians, the presence of big companies passed to represent a major risk to the community in which they are relocated - because, despite recruiting a large number of people at the start, their possible relocation passed to represent a huge social threat. Thus, large conglomerates have become blackmailers, sequestering a large number of people. In this way, those big companies are always negotiating special terms with their respective governments, and often these special conditions radically revert the benefits that they can represent - because they no longer refer to the benefits they can bring to the region, and start referring to the harm that a possible transfer to another place can unchain.

Globalization, concentration and speculation

Globalization and new media tend to generate high income concentration - and, always, high concentration inevitably leads to speculation. It is the scale what turns safer the risk and what produces the inevitable impulse to speculation in macroeconomic terms. High concentration of wealth always produces speculation. Speculation always generates turbulence.

Interest rates

Considering this scenario, we started observing what most governments around the world are doing. One of the most common elements we have found in the beginning of the third millennium is the general decline in interest rates. Firstly, such decline evidences a promiscuity between executive and legislative powers, eliminating much of the principle of their independence - one of the pillars of democracy. Many economists say that low interest rates encourage investment. But, in bad faith or ignorance, they do not say that everything depends on the scale. Below a certain level, very low interest rates annihilate savings and become, in fact, an instrument of transfer of capital from individuals to the State. It is not difficult to see that this process generates a greater concentration of income, the impoverishment of the population and consequent reduction in consumption. But governments, almost all of them, do not stop there. Almost all started practicing a generalized increase in taxes, which represents greater income concentration. They increase bureaucracy, increasing costs and creating turbulence.

Credit

But, as alleged attenuating, they distributed capital in

form of credit, simulating a situation of liquidity and generating debit. However, the inevitable inability to settle the loan creates deep dependence of people and a complete paralyzation after some time. On March 6, 2013, the New York Times published: As Fears Recede, Dow Industrials Hit a Milestone. In fact, Dow Jones returned to levels prior to the onset of the Great Recession of 2008. But with all information we know, it is evident that this is not about a stable structural condition. Surely it is just a peak in an environment of intense fluctuation and turbulence.

China war

Present structural conditions are terribly negative. We ask ourselves why politicians have done so much stupidity in the economic field. A possible answer is that it is about stupid people. But then we ask ourselves how so many stupid people can exist so generously distributed in so many countries? Here, the answer does not emerge with great clarity. In fact, it seems impossible that there are so many stupid people in so many places at once. But we know that China is orienting its capital to the deveopment of an aggressive army, its war navy and a future control of the orbital space. We also know, by simple deduction, that it is not possible for the US or Europe to launch a big bomb on China. We also know that the only real consumer markets in the world are the United States, Europe, together with Japan, Canada and Australia. Therefore, the economic strangulation of these markets - through laws establishing a dramatic reduction of liquidity - can represent a real bomb against China until that country effectively abandon its declared bellicose intentions. If not for this economic war, we would have the means to reverse the present disastrous situation.

Debit and confiscation

Firstly, it does not seem possible to settle the accumulated debt. Just to have an idea, in December 2012 it was announced that the overall debt of the United States may reach 80 trillion. Despite of such terrible scale, measures should be quickly adopted. Interest rate should rise - in late 2012, overnight was even banned by law in Europe! The ultra low interest rates (even negative real rates) in early 2013 represent, in reality, a transfer of capital from people to governments. In other words, they are nothing more than confiscation.

Frauds

The expansion of the monetary base is another problem - because it is disguised by frauds like the calculation of inflation (currently based on a small portion of consumption, not rarely subsidized by the State), and the GDP fraud (that now incorporates the spendings of the respective State, often unproductive, as income!!!).

What should be done

Taxes should dramatically go down in order to re-distribute the capital by society, and should rise to the big fortunes, but in a very gradual strategy: a rich person or company should never be discouraged in their aims. Banks and churches should start paying taxes (as well as politicians, when the case!). The relocation of production or of the company headquarters should be accompanied by a customs tax system, to consider the social situation in the different countries. Importation taxes should consider the social conditions of the exporting countries – and the product of those taxes should be reverted to the improvement of the relations between the respective countries and, when possible, to the improvement of the related social conditions. But none of this is being done. Thus, the only thing we can do is to wait for the abyss – even if we are not able to imagine what it will be.

Paying taxes

We read Italian newspapers and learned that politicians do not pay for virtually anything - taxpayers pay everything for them. Even ex-politicians receive large amounts of money from the State. In Greece such behavior was spread out through many sectors of the population. According to the media in Portugal, politicians have subsidized lavish lunches and dinners, as well as luxury cars among other benefits, when much of the population goes hungry. There, banks and the Church don't pay taxes. In Spain, we learn that all that also happens, and more. In Belgium, European politicians do not pay VAT and have many other benefits. In Washington DC the number of lobbyists who finance the pomp and circumstance of the political world has grown by an overwhelming order - indeed, it also happens in Belgium. But isn't such thing corruption?

Low cost

In Brazil, articles in newspapers denounce that the expenses of the governmental palace are much higher than those of the Buckingham Palace, with much of the population in poverty. In China, the New York Times was banned for denouncing the sudden and enormous enrichment of the Chinese leader. In Angola, a small group of people is among the world's richest, with a miserable population, thanks to the sale of oil to several countries, including China. This seems to be a general image worldwide. On the other hand, we witness not only a large concentration of income, a formidable increase of social asymmetry, but also as a rapid degeneration of the quality of products and services: it is the so-called "low cost." Everything is a bit worse, sometimes not so cheap.

Market and trust

In economic terms, what is the relationship between these two great waves? What generated the so-called "market value", in logical terms, had in itself certain operating principles. One of them was what we call "trust." Trust requires not only mutual, natural and automatic agreement, without the need of a formal contract, but also an approach of commitment to a community over a certain period of time. Hyper communication media in real time eliminated the time and with it trust and respect for others. It is not possible to exist respect when we have no time. A dead end? No! What generated trust was technology: the phonetic alphabet associated with paper. We should invent a new technology to produce a new mutation.

Representation

Our model of representative democracy – which presently designs nearly all democracies in the twenty-first century - began in the Roman world, about two thousand years ago. Representative democracy is that one in which people elected represent sets of people. That is, citizens elect their representatives, providing them with full powers to certain actions. Depending on the countries, these actions are more or less comprehensive. Representative democracy affects especially the executive and legislative powers. Why representative democracy started in ancient Rome? Because Rome was the first place in the world where phonetic alphabet associated with a flexible medium like papyrus allowed a huge territory with centralized control. In other words, people who were distant from the center of decision needed someone to represent them, as their rights or wishes could be considered by decision-makers. Beyond the physical distance, there was ignorance. People far from the center ignored the reality of the whole and could not accurately know what was possible or not.

Alexandria

This model of governance disappeared with the loss of control, on the part of Rome, of Alexandria - then the largest producer of papyrus at the time. Without that media, Roman world crumbled. Then, around the year 1,000, with the paper manufacturing in Europe and, later, with Gutenberg's movable metal type press, the European continent was gradually moving back towards a representative democracy inspired on Rome. This happened, gradually and increasingly widespread, in the nineteenth century.

Groups of interests

We are always talking about economy. The order of the structure of State's decision implies the possibility of adopting more or less efficient economic strategies. In this way, in the first half of the twentieth century, people's representatives still had a clear social function. But after the deployment of powerful telecommunication systems on a planetary scale, each person ceased to be away from the center, the center ceased to exist and people now have access to all information in real time. It is natural that in some places of the planet such is not the dominant reality yet, but in many countries this is the phenomenon that begins to impose itself more and more clearly. When this happens, the representatives simply cease to work and begin to gravitate - which is clearly denounced by the press every day - around the most varied kinds of interests.

The rule of politicians

Therefore, in Europe - like in the United States - people have questioned, sometimes with violence, about the present role of politicians. In the former system of democratic representation, representatives came out from the place they had lived, participated, not infrequently with very well defined professions. The professional politician did not exit yet. With the loss of function, the politician becomes professional - ie: nothing. He emerges as "professional of corridors", specialist in lunches and dinners, attentive to the interests surrounding him. Thus, we have lawyers or economists presidents or prime ministers who have never exercised their original profession and who know very little about them. Perhaps the only country in the world, in the beginning of the twentieth-first century, which does not belong to this perverse and degenerate system of representation, is Switzerland, with its direct democracy – that surely represents a serious threat to the existence of degenerated politicians around the world.

Cities

I remember that when I was a boy, New York was worldwide famous for being the city that had everything. If we looked for a store of scissors, hats, gloves, or whatever, very surely we would find it in New York City. Not only, it was a city with all kinds and sizes of bookstores and art galleries. I remember myself walking by Madison Avenue and visiting small and delightful contemporary art galleries. Today, virtually all them disappeared. New York has become a city without bookstores, with no diversity, with only large clothing stores, banks, drugstores and little else. Authorities say that it is the law of market working. But if market forces work wonderfully for the production of manufactured goods, food, clothing or appliances, the same cannot be said in relation to other areas - for a simple reason: the logical structure of human activities is not standard.

Big averages

Capitalism and market forces produce big averages. It is enough to visit a non-capitalist country to see clearly how this happens. In a country governed by the laws of the market all seem to benefit from large averages - is what led to the so-called "middle class." But other areas of human activity, such as health, art, education or culture do not work under broad averages. There is no average in health: you have or do not have health. In education and culture the medium is the root of the word mediocrity. Art simply does not exist on an average - when it is designed by an average, it becomes handicraft.

Laws of market and urban planning

Can a city - or a country – be exclusively governed by the laws of the market? Or, slightly changing the question: would market laws survive inside a homogeneous logical medium without diversity? What we see in such impulse for a broad average is the transformation of the whole city on the periphery, revolutionizing all theories of urbanism. You could say that, simply, it is about the reality of our time. But, if so, are we all condemned to a society without culture and without art? How consumption works when there is no longer questioning and discovery? More than that: is this the future we want? The journalist Bruno García Gallo, writing for the Spanish newspaper El País, in the edition of February 21, 2013, revealed a disturbing reality of the city of Madrid: the city is losing, in accelerated pace, everything related to culture. Only at the Gran Via, in a few years, almost all movie theaters disappeared, giving way to clothing stores. Madrid arts commissioner Fernando Villalonga lamented that people appear to be "more concerned about the fate of Palácio de la Música than about the 4,000 layoffs at Bankia," and continued, "...life goes on and the big movie theaters turn into something else, such is the course of history, we cannot keep up the same uses." But is this really the inevitable course of history?

Paris

One of the most notable examples to the contrary is the city of Paris. There, with a much smarter strategic vision, authorities dramatically cut taxes from business oriented to culture and art - result: the city flourishes with bookstores, art galleries, designer shops and so on. It is the city with the greatest flow of world tourism. Those establishments of culture keep the city alive, operating a continuous education of its citizens, attracting millions of visitors and, therefore, generating direct and indirect revenue.

Ghost cities

Instead, when the city is killed by the elimination of its cultural sector, in the name of the law of the market for everything, good part of the present and future market is also killed. When I see what has happened in these cities that are vandalized by taxes and bureaucracy, I wonder whether it might be time to establish some intelligence requirement for candidates for municipal leaders. Or at least that they should study a little of economy! How to react against so disturbing news? You can write, spread out what is happening, talk to your friends, make clear that your vote will be considered regarding such reality and so on. If you will not react, surely we will have soon our future urban spaces transformed into ghost cities.

Italy

There are things that do not depend on an immediate reality. One of those things is what we call governance. In February 2013 an unexpected situation appeared in Italy: after the election, with right and left wings with equal slices, no dialogue was possible because everything would be automatically locked by the other part: good or bad things. Thus, the so-called ungovernability appeared. What we should ask is whether, especially from an economic standpoint, such a ungovernability is desirable or not.

Ungovernability

To start, it is important to have in mind that it is about a partial ungovernability. Government continues existing, but it is no longer allowed to establish new laws, taxes and programs. It should continue the regular administration, without novelties. In 2012, everybody commented about the European disaster.

In that year, virtually all European countries walked into the abyss. But this did not happen with Belgium. As John Lanchester wrote an interesting article in the London Review of Books - the Belgian economy was one of the fastest growth in Europe, seven times more than the German economy. The reason soon became clear: Belgium had been without government for sixteen months. It is true that before Belgium had a considerable deficit and a large debt. But it was free to react, to grow and to pay its debit, because there was not a government creating new taxes or increasing the existing ones, establishing more and more bureaucratic procedures that would create more barriers for the development of the country. The State was not always such a declared destroyer of economies. Examples range from the Marshall Plan in Europe or even to the United States in several moments of its history. In 2013, when Italy announces itself almost ungovernable, stocks fall, panic emerge - but would not be better to be like that?

The function of the State

There are simple things in the world, but not infrequently hard to be understood. If the supreme function of the State is not to defend its citizens, what will be? We see a little everywhere the world in a terrible situation regarding to many individuals who lose their homes, become homeless, and many times true slaves for the rest of their lives with huge debts to financial systems. It is not, once again, a moral approach, but only a practical and objective one.

People and economy

Simply, those people cease being part of the market, and start to weigh on the economic system. Why does this happen? In Brazil there is an essential legal element, which should be applied universally: the so-called root-good. A "root-good" is the home of the family – if it is officially registered as such it immediately becomes unattainable, even by the State.

The reasoning is very simple: a family, children, old people, cannot be sacrificed by a criminal act of a financial gang, by a corrupted or incompetent government, or even by the irresponsibility of one of its own members. With root-good, when the financial system provides credit, it knows in advance and well that the property of the family is inalienable. This generates a key element for people in difficult situation to survive and re-start productive life. Thus, people can return to the market.

Repayment of the principal

Another important element that should be universal is the mandatory repayment of the principal of the debt by receiving the pawned goods. Today, in many countries, people lose their properties - that pass automatically to the financial system - and continue with the same debt they had before! But such is economically negative! Why people do not start a global movement of protest as to have these two legal elements, so simple and righteous, immediately applied?

Primitive

About thirty years ago the Mexican writer and poet Octavio Paz, Nobel Prize, reflected on the nature of the State and, inevitably, on its implications on economy. Even in classical antiquity there always was the belief, more or less present until now, on a purity and innocence of the primitive human being. Firstly, we forget that the classification "primitive" is a gross generalization in defense of historic civilization. When we speak about "primitive", are we talking about the human being of ten, fifty or a hundred thousand years ago? Homo sapiens sapiens - modern humans – exists at least since about two hundred thousand years ago.

Violence

When talking about economy we are always touching some kind of violence - because violence is nothing more than the expression par excellence of the thermodynamic mechanism. When things change, there is violence. Thus, there is no economy without violence. However, there are kinds of violence that are acceptable and others not - but such condition, to be or not acceptable, never depends on moral issues. It will be unacceptable if violence is characterized by a strong entropic nature; it will be acceptable if oriented towards negentropy. Generation of violence is only one: the rescue of identity.

Feed and memory

Any economic principle emerges from these principles: violence and identity. Thus, there is no purity or innocence in any human being or any living being. That's what shocks us when we see a lion killing a zebra. Quickly, we justify: but it was only about food. However, what alimentation is? Couldn't be, beyond physical alimentation, a spiritual one? - like what happens with humans? But, no one asks about memory. A lion kills a zebra as his food because his long-term memory system is not developed. It operates in flashes of reality, where the apparent continuous knows only a tenuous existence.

State and war

What is the role of the State? Octavio Paz argued that it was the preservation of peace among citizens and the unchain of war between other states. In this way, when we would not have more State, it would be the outbreak of violence between citizens. And Mr. Paz asks: if the abolition of the State triggers our return to a perpetual civil strife, how to avoid war? When Thoreau said that government is best which governs least, he added: when people will be prepared for it. Are we prepared for a life without the figure of the father who punishes and ensures peace at home? It is a question that overlaps an ostensive apparently unknown reality: it is the first time in the entire existence of homo sapiens that there is no longer any inhabited place on planet Earth: there is no longer any room for the conquest of territory. Everything is now definitively occupied by humans. Consequently, there is no longer any room for what we know as war. Would be conditions for war or State, as we have known in the last thousands of years? Simple euestions to reflect about: State, economy and violence.

Ignorance

We read newspapers. We watch the news on television, the debates... and what impresses us most? Something that can be summarized in just one word: incompetence. Next time you watch a television debate on the economic issues of your country, pay attention at the clothes people are wearing, their movements, the words they use, and their contradictions. You will be impressed by the low level of these people. We are so narcotized by the environment we live in, that we do not give attention to obvious things. But why do we have such incompetence so flagrant in our world? Why our politicians usually became the most obvious representation of ignorance and lack of competence?

Natural Selection

There are two answers... or two pertinent observations about this phenomenon. Firstly, the political

243

world has become a place of intense competition, of arduous concurrence. The most successful politicians are those who devoted more time to the corridors of power, to the lunches, dinners, and social meetings. Because everything is about a principle similar to that of the Natural Selection, over time, only those who had devoted all their time to such activities survived in the political world. Thus, they become people who, in fact (even though they could bear a diploma), never studied, did not have a profession, never worked on something productive.

Parasites

They became - as products of the System - in its parasites. Secondly, they were forced - also by the requirement of the System - to entice more voters - that is, their commodity-product. For this, also as part of the selection's gear, only those who had no limits to reach such objective could survive: what leads to corruption. We shouldn't forget that the words democracy and demagogy were born at the same time, together, in the ancient Greek universe. This does not mean that the politics should be eliminated. Politicians are, ultimately, all of us - who belong to the polis. What is important, is not stop reflecting.

Interest rates and savings

There are curious things in life. Interest rates fell, reaching zero or even negative values in real life. Media in general, scholars from universities (now often directly or indirectly involved in corruption scandals), and politicians proclaim: this is the best strategy to improve production and consumption. Strangely, nobody questions whether the radical lowering of interest rates is nothing more than a strategy of diverse States to be financed at free cost. Who pays the financing of states, of corrupt politicians and criminals, are all citizens and society. Furthermore, it encourages disastrous projects without consistency, because the risk is low. The lowering of interest rates beyond a certain limit not only funds criminals but also eliminates an essential element of Western society: savings. Since ancient Rome, savings have been an important element of the Western economy. When it ends? With the loss of the Roman control over the production of papyrus in Alexandria, and the early of the so-called Middle Ages.

Rumors

Despite the news, the world economic situation has not improved in recent weeks. It deteriorated even more. On February 20, 2013, the news was that the dramatic fall of gold and other commodities was due to "rumors" circulating in the Fed! Imagine a world market falling sharply due to rumors?! It makes no sense. This idea, that rumors move economies, is the result of what we call psychologism and that has caused major disasters throughout history. Whenever that happens, there is a picture of ignorance behind it.

Market risk

Then, yesterday, the U.S. network CNBC published an article according to which the true reason for the decline of gold and other commodities - but, paradoxically, also companies - was directly related to the end of the imminent danger of a fiscal cliff in the

United States, the end of the risk of Greece leaving the euro, and end pf the crisis in China! According to the article, as none of these dangers had happened (http://www.cnbc.com/id/100475489) gold fell as investors felt happy and comfortable, and were finally able to return to market risk. But everyone always knew that the fiscal cliff is just the tip of the iceberg in the United States and that it would never, by itself, represent the risk of a catastrophe; that Greece will never leave the euro if the euro continues to exist (to understand that it is enough to follow the dramatic situation in Spain, Portugal, Romania, Hungary or even in various sectors of France) - ie: nothing has changed here too; and the crisis in China ... a closed country, about which little is known, but where tension is always very high.

Freedom

That is: nothing of what was said makes sense. But it is important to look for a pattern of coherence in world movements. The G-20 Communiqué in Moscow - which ended in the last February 16 2013 - is very interesting. The world press, as if teleguided, focused this meeting as if it was dedicated to the present currency war. But one of the most alarming facts produced in that meeting was the strategic determination on the part of States to prevent companies to change their registered offices as to avoid the heavy tax burden imposed by governments, so many times corrupt. The idea is to block, increasingly, these movements, so as to compel companies and individuals to be subjected to terrible totalitarian and oppressive tax schemes. Gold, when it is not in certificates, also operates under the same logic. All this seems to fit perfectly in the strategy announced this week by the U.S. government - which has already being worked on for a long time - about a common market with Europe: all heading for a super control and constant surveillance. Since nothing has changed for the better, the banks virtually ceased to exercise their traditional role, and that even the overnight was banned by law (!). In Europe, we will see a turnaround within some time, with an expressive improvement of the value of gold.